抛 Turning Bricks into Jade

砖 引 玉

Critical Incidents for Mutual Understanding among Chinese and Americans

Mary Margaret Wang,
Richard W. Brislin,
Wei-zhong Wang,
David Williams, and
Julie Haiyan Chao

INTERCULTURAL PRESS ·
A Nicholas Brealey F

BOSTON ·

D0865070

First published by Intercultural Press, a Nicholas Brealey Publishing Company, in 2000. For information contact:

Intercultural Press
a division of
Nicholas Brealey Publishing
100 City Hall Plaza, Ste. 501
Boston, MA 02108, USA
Tel: 617-523-3801
Fax: 617-523-3708
www.interculturalpress.com

© 2000 by Intercultural Press

Nicholas Brealey Publishing
3-5 Spafield Street
Clerkenwell
London, EC1R 4QB, UK
Tel: +44-207-239-0360
Fax: +44-207-239-0370
www.nicholasbrealey.com

ISBN-13: 978-1-877864-81-0
ISBN-10: 1-877864-81-1

Printed in the United States of America

11 10 09 08 07   6 7 8 9 10

Library of Congress Cataloging-in-Publication Data
Turning bricks into jade: critical incidents for mutual understanding among Chinese and Americans / Mary M. Wang...[et al.].
    p. cm.
  Includes bibliographical references and index.
  ISBN 1-877864-81-1
    1. United States—Relations—China. 2. China—Relations—United States. 3 United States—Ethnic relations. 4. Chinese—United States—social life and customs. 5. Chinese—social life and customs 6. Americans—China—social life and customs. 7. Intercultural communication—United States. 8. Intercultural communication—China. I. Wang, Mary M.
E183.8.C5 T856 2000
303.48'273051—dc21
                                                    00–040731

Table of Contents

Acknowledgments

This book would not have been possible without the assistance of the following people who took the time to participate as members of our validation sample. Some of these individuals also offered suggestions for incidents or made additional—sometimes lengthy—comments in the course of the validation, which were then incorporated into the explanations. We are very grateful to each one of them for lending us their expertise.

Grace Auyang, Sara Banaszak, Kim Bench, Troy Bench, Lauren Bickart-Zhang, Kevin Bishop, Wendy Bishop, Laura Burian, Dan Chay, Heidi Chay, Jeff Cirillo, Elizabeth Dahl, Linell Davis, Haybina Hao, Jeffrey Hayden, Nancy Hilty, Daw-jing Hsiung, Hsingyi (Ruby) Huang, Bijun Li, Jengchen Li, Meina W. Liu, Ye Liu, Li Lu, Xiaojing (Lynette) Shi, Jinglei (Jerry) Wang, Tingyu Wang, Xin Wang, Yue Wang, Brian Wannerman, Nancy Wong, Fengyu Yang, Xingchen (Robert) Ye, Daniel Ping Young, Xiaomin Yu, Zhenghong Yu, Ziying Zhao, Willis Zumwalt, Yi Zhou, and two individuals who for personal reasons chose not to be identified by name.

We would also like to thank Randy Chiu, Yadong Luo, Xiang Xu, and Xiaohui Zhu for clarifying information that led to some of the material in our discussions of incidents, and Dan Xie for suggesting the title.

Introduction

What Is Culture?

Culture includes so many things (values, traditions, ideals of behavior, expectations, even cuisine, art, and theater) that it can often be used by one person in a discussion to mean one thing, and by others in the same discussion to mean others. Before we can discuss specific aspects of Chinese and American cross-cultural encounters, we need to define what we mean by the term *culture*. In his 2000 book *Understanding Culture's Influence on Behavior*, Richard Brislin provides a useful list of features that define what we mean when we speak of culture, particularly in the context of cross-cultural interaction. We summarize them briefly here in an effort to clarify some of the goals of these materials.

Culture is the human-made part of the environment. Culture can be distinguished from climate and environment. People come up with ways of responding to the environment in which they find themselves; those responses are part of their culture, but the environment itself is not.

Culture reflects widely shared assumptions about life. People who are from the same culture will share values, ideals, and assumptions about what constitutes appropriate behavior. In short, they will generally agree about what is a proper response to a new situation and what is "simply not done."

Culture is so fundamental that most people do not and cannot discuss or analyze it. Because culture is the assumptions about what gives life meaning, the shared ideals and values of a society, people find it difficult to stand back and describe the basics of their culture. Everything about one's own culture seems "normal." When people are asked to

1

explain something about their culture to someone from another culture, they are often at a loss, since they have never had occasion to think about what to them is simply "the way things are."

Culture becomes evident through "well-meaning clashes." Because most people have never really thought about their own culture any more than they think about the individual motions they make to walk across a room, they tend to take notice of culture only when they encounter people from other countries who are behaving in a socially inappropriate way, deviating from their own cultural norms. In such "well-meaning clashes," the people involved are trying to be polite and respectful, yet their different cultural conditioning leads them to manifest good behavior differently. Cultural clashes of this kind have a lasting impact on participants and observers, often causing them to examine their own behavior and culturally conditioned responses.

Culture is transmitted from generation to generation. Through experience, children learn what is valued in their culture and what is proscribed. Adults are often able to remember and describe specific incidents and experiences in their childhood through which they became aware of certain cultural norms and expectations. Role models for acceptable and unacceptable behavior are pointed out to children to show them what happens to those who embrace, or fail to embrace, values and behaviors acceptable in their society. In this way, culture is passed on from one generation to the next.

Culture allows people to fill in the blanks. Given almost any situation, even quite a novel one, people can fill in the blanks as to what is expected in their own culture. Take the example of the individual whose friend's spouse dies suddenly. Even though this exact event has never occurred before, the example of elders on similar occasions in the past, stories read or heard, examples from movies, friends' experiences, and many other subtle and unremembered sources guide behavior so that one knows just the right things to do. If people have such an experience while living in another culture, however, they will generally find themselves at a loss.

Cultural values endure. While modernization or changes in styles of living may seem to occur very rapidly, fundamental cultural shifts take place slowly, over a number of generations. Cultural values and the sense of what is acceptable and what is not persist in the face of alterations in lifestyle. Any suggestion that a change in cultural values would be a good thing is likely to be met with much opposition. An example in the United States is the right to bear arms. While there are many who would like to limit this right, it will not happen quickly or easily because there are too many people for whom gun ownership is fundamental to the culture. An example from China is the failure of the Cultural Revolution to eradicate the use of hierarchical forms of address; a decade of calling everyone "comrade" was simply too short a time to effect a lasting change on a set of behaviors that reflected deeply held cultural values.

Violations of cultural norms have emotional impact. When people see a violation of their cultural norms by someone from their own or another culture, they will tend to feel angry or upset. Violations of cultural norms are described as "rude" or "stupid," not as "curious" or "intriguing." The well-meaning clashes mentioned earlier are memorable, in part, because of their emotional impact.

Cultural differences can easily be set in contrast. One hears generalizations like "North Americans tend to be far more concerned about punctuality than are South Americans" or "Japanese people make refusals much more indirectly than Americans do." It is often convenient and easy to describe culture in terms of what seem like opposite approaches in two different cultures. These oppositions center around things such as attitudes toward time, personal space, authority figures, and institutions.

Cross-Cultural Training

The Purpose of This Book

Like all cross-cultural training materials, these critical incidents were created to promote success in overseas assignments, specifically those involving Americans and Chinese. The purpose of this book is to present a set of cross-cultural training materials that will be useful to Americans who have accepted assignments in China or to Chinese who have accepted assignments in the United States. The materials should be equally beneficial to Chinese who will work closely with Americans in China and to Americans who will have extensive contact with Chinese in the United States. It is likely that parts of this book will also prove helpful to people from other countries such as Canada, Singapore, Hong Kong, Taiwan, and much of Western Europe. Most of the critical incidents take place in a workplace or academic setting, so they will be most useful to people who have accepted assignments in those contexts. They should also be of more limited benefit to people who are operating in a health-care setting, who are trying to break into the entertainment industry, or whose main purpose is travel.

The Goals of Cross-Cultural Training Programs

Training should help people achieve success in an overseas assignment according to four criteria. Attention to these four goals helps cross-cultural trainers select relevant materials for their programs and helps trainees focus on issues they will face in their future job assignments.

To enjoy overseas assignments and benefit from them. Many people enjoy new and different activities in the short term or during the early part of an overseas assignment. This stage can often generate the excitement of going on a vacation where every experience is satisfying because it is new or different. However, enjoying an overseas assignment goes beyond that. It is the general feeling of well-being that people get who are doing something worthwhile, not just for their careers but also in terms of personal growth. This includes developing successful interpersonal relationships with host nationals. Reaching this level of enjoyment and benefit is an indication of success in an overseas assignment and by anyone's standard can be called "an intercultural experience" rather than "a trip."

To have hosts reciprocate this enthusiasm. The positive feelings cannot be one-sided. It is possible for the sojourners to have positive feelings while their hosts feel that they are not productive or helpful. Sojourners might be meeting their own goals; however, their hosts may feel that they have gained nothing from their foreign guests' presence. Hosts should feel that they have benefited from the sojourners' contributions. They should feel that they are better off not just because of the work the foreign guests accomplish but also because of the new ideas and methods that they introduce. New ideas and ways of doing things can often be more beneficial to the hosts because their influence can last long after the sojourners leave.

To achieve one's goals. Almost all sojourners have tasks associated with their overseas assignments: international students want to obtain university degrees, or at least course credit; overseas businesspeople want to establish joint ventures; and technical advisers want to introduce new development projects. Successful cross-cultural assignments mean that sojourners accomplish their tasks in a reasonable amount of time after some inevitable adjustment and integration of cultural differences into their work plans. Ideally, the tasks should not take longer than they would take back in the home country (Brislin and Yoshida 1994).

To reduce stress. After a predictable period of time (approximately six months) during which they experience the psychological upheaval and anxiety stemming from culture shock, sojourners should experience no more stress than they would in their own culture (Brislin and Yoshida). Culture shock can be reduced if its causes are understood (e.g., frustrations with time delays, Levine 1997), and cross-cultural training can include material on these causes.

American and Chinese Conceptions of Cross-Cultural Training

Americans and Chinese hold different attitudes toward cross-cultural training. A few comments about cross-cultural training in the United States and China should help put the materials provided here into perspective.

The United States. Cross-cultural training is an accepted concept in the United States, and general texts that deal with employee training and development often contain sections on cross-cultural training (Noe 1999). However, there is no guarantee that organizations that have selected people for overseas assignments will offer this type of training. There are many competitors for an organization's training budget, such as computer use, leadership, public speaking, marketing skills, and so forth. In some companies, there is still the attitude that good business practice is pretty much the same all over the world and that cultural differences are minimal and need no special attention. It is our observation that the decision to budget for cross-cultural training is often made by executives who themselves have lived in other cultures. They know what it is like to adjust to cultural differences and know that even if there are general global business principles, the manner in which they are applied is influenced by culture. The executives' attitudes toward cross-cultural training are affected by their own personal experiences (Eagly and Chaiken 1998). There is now an extensive published literature on cross-cultural training (e.g., Landis and Brislin 1983; Fowler and Mumford 1995, 1999; Landis and Bhagat 1996; Kohls and Brussow 1995), although a disproportionate percentage of the contributors to the literature are from North America. There is general acceptance that good cross-cultural training programs can benefit participants in developing good relationships with hosts, decreasing debilitating culture shock, improving job effectiveness, and completion of assignments rather than premature termination (Brislin and Yoshida).

China. Training for skill development is highly valued by success-ful Chinese managers. Oded Shenkar (1990) uses the term *personal training* to refer to formal programs that increase managerial skills. A group of successful Chinese managers who were studied perceived per-sonal training as the most important element in their success and wanted to spend more time on it. Managers make great efforts to take time from their managerial responsibilities for personal training, and selec-tion for training programs is seen as a reward for past excellence in job performance.

There are two important reasons why managers in China value personal training so highly. First, similar to managers in other coun-tries, they find it is the only way to keep up with state-of-the-art tech-nologies and to keep informed about the rapidly changing world eco-nomic situation. As China moves toward a truly open market economy, there will be an ever-greater need for managers to continuously im-prove their knowledge and skills to be competitive. As commercial ac-tivities between China and the rest of the world increase, managers will see firsthand the great necessity to understand cultural differences and ways of doing business with their counterparts in other countries.

Another reason for Chinese managers' desire for personal training is that hard work is one of the most important determinants of career success. "A manager who pursues personal training diligently was looked upon as a hard-working individual, thereby winning the respect of his supervisors and colleagues" (Stewart and Him 1990, 63).

Cross-cultural training, however, is not as well developed as it is in North America, Europe, or Japan. Usually training in foreign languages and functional managerial skills is available in China. Although manag-ers understand the importance of studying cultural backgrounds to com-municate with their business partners effectively, extensive training is rarely available in the country. The government does provide short training sessions for people who go abroad for public affairs. The train-ing helps participants learn foreign languages and understand social skills and appropriate behavior in other countries. Also, some foreign companies operating in China are beginning to offer cross-cultural train-ing to Chinese employees who work with expatriate managers.

In cross-cultural training, as in formal schooling, the Chinese tend to put great emphasis on paper credentials. Consequently, a diploma or a certificate will often be more convincing to employers and co-workers than will actual skills acquired. This tends to be especially true in areas where assessing the quality of training is more difficult. For example, students who wish to go to English-speaking countries to study will often expend a great deal of energy on getting a high TOEFL (Test of English as a Foreign Language, required by most U.S. colleges and universities for admission) score but will neglect to develop speaking and writing skills that will be necessary for their success in their studies (but not tested on the TOEFL). A high TOEFL score is seen by the Chinese as an assurance of competence in English, even when the person who achieved that score is virtually unable to express himself or herself in English. When high-quality training programs are available, however, and when people are able to see that graduates of such programs are truly more competent than others, the emphasis on paper credentials may diminish somewhat. An example would be the fields of engineering and computer science, where competence is more easily measured against objective criteria. We predict that managers and professionals in China will be pleased to see more efficient formal programs developed in areas such as cross-cultural training.

Critical Incidents and Culture Assimilators

The materials in this book are a set of critical incidents, comprising a culture-specific culture assimilator.

History and Development

Critical incidents have been used in cross-cultural training since the early 1960s (Wight 1995). Fred E. Fiedler, Harry C. Triandis, Charles Osgood, and Lawrence Stolurow, working together at the University of Illinois, are generally credited with developing the first culture assimilator, though Triandis insists that the idea was Stolurow's (Triandis 1995a). The four were looking for ways to improve "intercultural communication, interaction, leadership and training" (179). Since that time critical incidents have been used to help many different types of people prepare for a wide range of assignments: businesspeople, students, diplomats, technical advisers, Peace Corps volunteers, and others. They have proven helpful in facilitating cooperation in the workplace between African American and European American employees and in training health-care professionals to better serve their diverse clients.

Definition of Critical Incidents

A critical incident is essentially a story involving two or more well-meaning characters from different cultures. As the story unfolds, readers are given various bits of useful information for interpreting the story, or incident. The conclusion generally involves a misunderstanding among the people involved in the story or a sense of bewilderment concerning what happened in spite of the fact that the characters involved were attempting to behave in culturally appropriate ways given the norms of the country in which the incidents take place.

Critical incidents are, in fact, very like the stories that sojourners tell about the experiences they and their acquaintances have with the host culture. Travelers in a foreign land don't say "I encountered a most interesting example of the importance of maintaining vertical relationships in a hierarchical society today"; they tell a story about how awkward they felt when a student or subordinate behaved in a way they found too formal or obsequious, and how the subordinate then attempted to explain his or her behavior to them. They don't talk in the abstract about the implications of cultural differences in courtship behaviors; they tell stories about the guy who got himself into a real jam by asking his roommate's sister to go for a walk during an evening dance party. The essence of a critical incident is that individuals behaving with the best intentions and all the cultural sensitivity they can muster end up confused and unhappy about the interaction as a result of cultural differences that they do not fully understand.

The best critical incidents capture an important concept that is useful when thinking about, adjusting to, and interacting in other cultures. Examples of these concepts are provided in the critical incidents involving people, their behavior, their interactions with others, their possible misunderstandings, and possible recoveries from the misunderstandings. A concept without an example often fails to find a permanent place in a person's memory, since the concept's importance is unclear and there is nothing concrete to which to attach it. There are many important and useful concepts for people adjusting to other cultures, but without specific and compelling examples, people may not internalize them. On the other hand, examples of behaviors in other cultures that do not have a concept attached to them may fade from memory over time. There are so many examples of everyday behaviors in which people engage that nobody can remember them all. The combination of a concept and a compelling example is more likely to be remembered than is either element by itself.

An example of a critical incident combined with an important concept should make our argument clearer. This short incident centers around an experience that is common to Americans sojourning in China.

Norman Tate was the vice president of a farm equipment manufacturer whose headquarters was in Chicago, Illinois. He traveled to Shanghai on a six-month assignment to investigate the possibilities of expansion into Chinese markets. One day he read an article in the newspaper based on an interview with a government official who dealt with agriculture, Lu Kang. Norman found Mr. Lu's phone number and called for an appointment, since he thought there would be concerns of mutual interest. Mr. Lu took the call, but he was clearly uncomfortable speaking with Norman. The phone call did not lead to an appointment for a face-to-face meeting. Did Norman do something wrong?

The short answer is yes. In China, people who do not know each other use intermediaries far more often than people in the United States do. In Chicago and other American cities, Norman can make a "cold call": he can call someone whom he does not know on the phone and ask for an appointment. If the person called feels that Norman sounds like a sensible person and gives good reasons for the suggested appointment, a meeting is likely to be scheduled. In China Norman should work through an intermediary, someone both he and Mr. Lu know and trust. The intermediary speaks for Norman, and since Mr. Lu trusts the intermediary, an appointment will probably be scheduled.

Our argument is that the combination of critical incident (the story) and important concept (use of intermediaries) makes this example memorable and useful. In addition, understanding the concept often leads to guidelines for success. Here, the guidance is to seek out an intermediary who will place a call to Mr. Lu.

Definition of Culture Assimilators

When cross-cultural trainers prepare a large number of critical incidents and organize them to communicate various important points about culture and cultural differences, the result can be called a culture assimilator (Fiedler, Mitchell, and Triandis 1971; Cushner and Brislin 1996).*

The term *culture assimilator* does not comes from one of the ways

---

* Rosita D. Albert (1983) suggested the name *intercultural sensitizer* (ICS), since *culture assimilator* seemed to her to suggest that trainees would be expected to take on the target culture and forget their own culture. She has since withdrawn this criticism, because she has found that the culture assimilator also makes trainees more aware of *their own* cultural conditioning and the effect that it has on their behavior and on their responses to the behavior of culturally different others (Albert 1995). Both terms are used.

to adjust to another culture; rather, it comes from the concept that people can slowly assimilate information about other cultures to aid in their achievement of the four criteria of success discussed on pages 4–5.

In the culture assimilator each incident is followed by a number of alternative explanations (usually four or five) of what happened. These alternative explanations are sometimes called *attributions* (Triandis 1995a), since each reflects different attributions that might be made about the behavior of one or more of the characters depending on the upbringing and cultural conditioning of the person doing the explaining. More than one of the alternatives can help in the explanation, especially when the multiple views of people from different cultures are presented. In other words, there might be two alternatives that are "good" choices, a third that is "on the right track," and a fourth (and fifth) that are "poor" choices. For some incidents, there will be one answer that is clearly better than all the others; for other incidents, there may be no answers that are completely off base. Again, this mirrors the experience of foreign sojourners. When members of two different cultures find themselves in conflict, the cause of the conflict is sometimes crystal clear to people who are familiar with both cultures. In other cases, those same people will differ somewhat as to their interpretations of what happened. This is especially likely to be the case if the cultural informants are from different cultures.

Think about what happens when a sojourner is caught in a cross-cultural misunderstanding. The sojourner and the native of the culture both go off and tell the story to their friends, who offer more or less insightful explanations of what happened. The best explanations accurately describe the attributions made by both parties. Less helpful alternatives are offered by well-meaning but culturally uninformed friends who tend to see the point of view of one side but misrepresent the point of view of the other side, or who make an inaccurate but plausible stab at explaining the behavior of the person from the other culture.

In the culture assimilator format, discussions of each alternative explanation are presented in a separate section. These discussions present aspects of culture and cultural differences that are relevant to each particular incident. The discussions make it possible for readers to use the culture assimilator on their own, and they help trainers to think about situations they may not have experienced themselves.

Culture-Specific and Culture-General Assimilators

There are two types of culture assimilators: culture specific and culture general. A culture-general assimilator (Cushner and Brislin) is designed to help people adjust to any other culture in which they might find themselves. Issues covered are therefore *general:* feelings of anxiety, negotiating ingroup and outgroup barriers, challenges to attributional processes, confrontations with value differences, and so forth. Culture-specific assimilators deal with the adjustment of people from one designated culture interacting with people from a second designated culture (Triandis 1995a). There are advantages and disadvantages to each type of assimilator, and a training program often uses both types. Because they are potentially of widespread use, culture-general assimilators can attract the attention of commercial publishers. However, the specificity needed for people adjusting to the actual culture in which they will be living is, by definition, absent. A culture-general assimilator can be useful in helping those who will deal with individuals from a variety of cultures to become more sensitive to the issues common to cross-cultural interactions; it is not as useful for preparing individuals for a sojourn to a specific culture.

Culture-specific assimilators can deal with very precise information about a country and the special issues facing people from another country who live in or interact with people from the first country. However, these too can be of limited use. For example, a culture assimilator for Anglo Americans who accept assignments in the Navajo nation in Arizona (Salzman 1990) may be extremely helpful to some people but not lend itself to extensive use outside the American Southwest. Given what might be called this "precise usefulness," widespread distribution of culture-specific materials is hindered when publishers point out that the potential market for culture-specific materials is small. Culture-specific assimilators are generally available through informal networks of cross-cultural trainers or through specialized libraries, such as those maintained by the Peace Corps (see Albert 1995 for information on some of these informal networks).

Why Use a Culture Assimilator?

The culture assimilator is valued as a training tool for its flexibility, its efficiency, and its ability to mimic the reality of cross-cultural interaction. It has a solid research base as well as being grounded in attribution theory and in theories of how people learn.

A culture assimilator provides trainees with a wide range of virtual experiences in a culture without the attendant dangers and discomforts of actually having those experiences. Trainees are free to make cultural blunders without jeopardizing the success of their sojourn and to come to their own conclusions about how they might better handle such incidents in real life. Through interaction with the materials in the culture assimilator, trainees become more aware of their own reactions in various situations and the attitudes that cause them to have those reactions. They learn to identify behaviors and responses in themselves that are personal and idiosyncratic; at the same time they become conscious of culturally conditioned responses they may make. Albert explains that the use of critical incidents in culture assimilators "focuses on differences in perceptions and interpretations of behaviors, differences which are important to the success of intercultural encounters yet difficult for the trainee to observe directly" (Albert 1995, 158).

Flexibility and Efficiency

As a training tool, the culture assimilator is flexible and efficient in terms of the number of trainees, time available for training, the experience necessary for both trainees and trainers who wish to use it, and the range of situations it allows trainees to experience.

Sojourners who find themselves about to embark on a foreign assignment with little time for preparation will value a culture-specific assimilator. The variety of incidents provides such sojourners with a good representation of the experiences they might expect to have in the foreign culture without the embarrassment or negative outcomes that accompany real-world errors. In the absence of a trainer, they will still have access to expert advice in the form of the explanations for the alternatives to each incident. Sojourners can work at their own pace either before they leave, on the plane en route to their assignments, or a few weeks after arrival when culture shock becomes a strong motivational force to find out more about the host culture and what is happening to them.

If an individual sits down with a culture assimilator and reads from the first page to the last, the total amount of time spent would be approximately five to seven hours. It's obviously not ideal to use the materials in this way, since there isn't much time for new ideas to be assimilated, but for a sojourner under pressure in an unfamiliar culture, the culture assimilator might be the best training available. A tremendous variety of possible experiences and theoretical concepts important to an understanding of the host culture would still have been covered in that very short period of time, and of course that person can always return to the materials later.

The culture assimilator is also useful when time is plentiful. If groups of trainees are reading each incident and discussing it at length, role-playing some of the incidents, and receiving lectures on related material from trainers, the culture assimilator can be used effectively over a period of days or weeks. Trainees can also be assigned individual incidents to do on their own between training sessions, to cover more in less time.

Furthermore, there is virtually no upper limit to the number of trainees who can work together with a culture assimilator. Some of the ways trainers can use the culture assimilator with a large group will be discussed in the next section.

The most commonly mentioned advantage of employing critical incidents in cross-cultural training is their usefulness in helping people with little or no previous cross-cultural experience to develop the ability to make *isomorphic attributions.* By this we mean that trainees learn to react to an incident as the people in the target culture would react to it; they learn to see and interpret incidents as the culturally different individuals in the incident would see them. By sensitizing trainees to the reasons for their own perceptions of and reactions to situations, the culture assimilator helps both naive and cross-culturally experienced trainees appreciate the point of view of individuals from the target culture. In addition, the explanations of the alternatives for each incident include discussions of theoretical concepts that can be especially useful to more experienced trainees.

While any training is ideally conducted by trainers who are well versed in the subject matter, the culture assimilator has the advantage of being less dependent on trainer expertise than many other training methods and materials. Because the culture-specific expertise is, so to speak, built into the explanations of the alternatives, experienced cross-cultural trainers should be able to use a culture-specific assimilator effectively without a deep knowledge of the target culture. This quality of the culture assimilator is, of course, very important to sojourners who wish to use a culture assimilator on their own.

A final reason to use culture assimilators in cross-cultural training is their demonstrated effectiveness. More research has been done on culture assimilators than on any other cross-cultural training method, and that research documents a number of positive outcomes. Culture assimilators have been shown to be effective in increasing the complexity of people's thinking, improving problem solving, bettering relations with hosts, and introducing behaviors that are appropriate in the host culture.[†]

How to Use Culture Assimilators in Cross-Cultural Training

How one uses a culture assimilator will depend, among other factors, on whether the individual will use the materials on his or her own or whether they will be incorporated into group training.

Individual Use

Some sojourners do not have the luxury of formal training sessions before they embark on a foreign assignment. The culture assimilator is particularly well suited to be of use to such travelers. An individual using a culture assimilator on his or her own proceeds in approximately the same way that a group with a trainer would. First, the sojourner reads each incident carefully, looking for clues in the behavior and reactions of the characters that might explain the resultant confusion or misunderstanding. Next, the reader looks over the four or five possible alternative explanations and selects the one he or she thinks best answers the question or challenge posed at the end of the incident, then checks the accuracy of his or her choice against the explanations found elsewhere in the material.

Some trainers and individuals prefer a linear format for considering the alternative attributions. This can be done by using a scale like that used for validating the incidents (see page 23). Readers then rate all possible alternatives, from "I am certain that this is correct" to "I am certain this is not correct."

[†] For a more thorough discussion of the research into culture assimilators and the ways in which they help trainees meet the criteria for success discussed previously (pages 4–5), see the Appendix.

When a group is involved in training, time is better spent in discussion and in the exchange of ideas and experiences than in writing out responses to incidents. However, keeping a journal of written responses to incidents and thoughts about the possible alternatives to look back on later in the sojourn can be very useful for people working on the materials in isolation. It can be very encouraging to return to both the culture assimilator and the notes made a year or eighteen months earlier to see the progress that has been made toward a greater understanding of the target culture.

Use by Cross-Cultural Trainers

Using a culture assimilator with a group of trainees need not differ much from using the material on one's own, though obviously there are more options available for enhancing the material with a group. Essentially, the incidents need to be presented and conclusions need to be drawn about the most suitable responses. The simplest way to proceed is to divide trainees into groups of at least four and no more than six or seven and ask them to read one or more incidents, discuss the alternative solutions, and then agree on one (or more).

Other options for presenting the incidents to trainees include assigning the reading of some or all incidents before the training course begins. Trainees may be asked to make some limited written response or simply to be prepared to discuss their conclusions. Alternatively, while a training course is in progress, of course, it is also possible to assign one or more incidents to be read before the next session.

Another popular method of presenting incidents is to give groups of trainees several incidents concerned with the same theme.‡ Trainees can then be given between twenty minutes and an hour, depending on the complexity of the incidents and the experience of the trainees, to come up with a consensus on the best explanation for each incident and to identify the underlying theme. Through a spokesperson, trainees can then report back to the large group. Trainees can be assigned the same group of incidents or different incidents concerned with different themes. This approach works especially well with trainees who may have considerable cross-cultural experience but perhaps not with the particular target culture.

---

‡ A list of themes and incidents that deal with those themes can be found on pages 235–36.

An alternative that is probably best used only occasionally is to present the incident in the form of a role play performed in front of the whole group. The role play can be done by trainees who have prepared in advance, but it is perhaps better handled by the trainer and the trainer's assistant(s). Such role plays have the advantage of being more vivid than written materials, but the setting and some of the psychological background of the incident that can be provided in writing may be lacking. Some trainers prefer to have groups of trainees read each incident, then role-play it, and finally discuss it. This is only possible if there is ample time, but it does go one step further toward putting trainees in the position of a sojourner experiencing the target culture.

A strong word of caution about role plays: it is essential to stick closely to the agreed-upon script and to have a rule that there will be no surprises. Role playing can become very emotional, triggering unpleasant memories or intense emotional reactions that must be resolved before training can continue. Critical incidents intentionally include an element of discomfort and confusion; it is unwise to attempt to intensify that negative or discomfiting affective element. Even when everything has been agreed on in advance, trainees may find themselves unexpectedly upset by immersing themselves to such an extent in an awkward, uncomfortable situation.

Discussion of the incidents can be handled in a number of different ways. Some trainers like to keep a tally of the choices made by individuals or groups on newsprint or an erasable board. Others simply allow spokespersons from each group to make an oral report.

Most trainers will want to lead a follow-up discussion (perhaps with the assistance of cultural informants from the target culture) in which the trainees' responses are analyzed and their questions answered. In our experience, trainees often want to reject all of the offered alternatives in favor of one of their own, based on their experiences with the target culture or with another culture that is familiar to them and has similarities to the target culture under study (e.g., another collectivist society). Discussion of the viability of such alternative explanations, or disagreement about the preferred alternative, can clarify conceptual issues or illuminate cultural differences that are still imperfectly understood. Discussion also offers the trainer the opportunity to remind trainees of individual differences within a culture.

If there is adequate time in a training program, we recommend combining the use of culture assimilators with other approaches. Lectures and readings on key theoretical concepts can be effectively alternated with the critical incidents. Once trainees have "experienced" conflict through the critical incidents, they are more receptive to hearing or reading about related theories. Simulations and situational exercises can also be used to enhance assimilator-based training.

Cross-cultural trainers using these materials need to keep in mind a few basic points. First, trainees need to be made aware that critical incidents do not have "right" and "wrong" answers, but the various alternatives are more or less helpful in explaining the well-meaning clash that occurred in the incident.

Second, trainers need to remind trainees frequently that not all individuals in a culture manifest cultural conditioning in quite the same way. One individual in a culture may demonstrate her respect for her elders by traveling overseas for five years to earn an advanced degree at a prestigious foreign university, thereby bringing honor to her parents and grandparents. Another individual may demonstrate respect for her elders by refusing such an opportunity and staying close to home where she can take care of her parents and grandparents on a day-to-day basis. Critical incidents can help trainees become aware of some of the ways cultural conditioning manifests itself in a society, but they need to keep an open mind when encountering similar incidents in training or in the real world. A related issue that should be made clear is that there are people in every society who do not fit the norm in every regard. Whereas the Chinese in general tend to be more collectivistic and the Americans in general tend to be more individualistic, one encounters markedly individualistic Chinese from time to time, and one may meet Americans who are extremely collectivistic.

Finally, although culture assimilators have been shown to be useful in getting trainees to move beyond stereotypes, selecting just a few incidents may have the opposite effect. Assimilators tend to repeat themes, presenting a number of similar incidents that differ in important but subtle ways having to do with context, the relative age of the characters, gender, and other factors. *It is best to use most or all of the incidents in a culture assimilator to avoid stereotyping or overgeneralization.* It is not, however, necessary to cover the incidents in the order in which they are presented. Each incident is complete in itself and does not presuppose knowledge of any other incident unless specified. Readers should feel free to start with any setting that interests them and to jump to another part of the book if they feel so inclined. Within each part incidents are arranged by increasing complexity, but that should not prevent readers from skipping around.

The Creation of These Incidents: A Culture-Specific Assimilator for China

Richard Brislin, Mary Wang, Wei-zhong Wang, and David Williams began meeting in the spring of 1994. At the time, all of us were involved with the East-West Center at the University of Hawaii in Honolulu. (Julie Haiyan Chao joined the project after the validation was complete.) We felt that due to increased interactions among American and Chinese businesspeople, educators, and students, a culture-specific assimilator was called for.

The incidents collected in this book take place mainly in academic and business settings. It is our intention and expectation that most users of these materials will be Chinese and North Americans who expect to be interacting primarily in one or both of these two settings. In other words, businesspeople, educators, and students will benefit most from these materials. However, because there are some experiences that are inevitable and because the differences in culture and expectations that lead to cross-cultural conflict and misunderstanding tend to be similar from one situation to another, we believe that this book will also be very useful to diplomats, volunteer workers, social service providers, and those who plan to travel extensively.

These materials are the result of a highly collaborative effort by people with a wide range of experiences in both cultures. Even though the story in an incident was often based on a real-life occurrence, the incidents themselves were revised and refined over weeks and months. The incidents, the alternative answers, and the explanations are based on the perspectives of all five authors, informed by their diverse socialization and experiences in both cultures.

Anyone familiar with other culture assimilators will soon notice that the incidents in this collection are longer and more complex than those in other assimilators (as discussed in Albert 1995). The authors made the decision to move toward complexity given our experiences: misunderstandings between Chinese and Americans are complicated and demand complex analyses. We felt that simplifying the real experiences on which many of the incidents in this book are based in an effort to focus on just one cultural contrast would have confused readers more than helped them. Interactions between Chinese and Americans are rarely simple; *there is almost never just one thing going on.* American individualism, for example, gives rise to notions about ownership that are very puzzling to the collectivist Chinese. Differences in how romance in the workplace is handled are related to differences in attitudes toward hierarchies and to collectivists' and individualists' differing perceptions of what one's own business is and what everyone else's business is. These issues cannot be easily separated from each other, nor should they be.

One result of this complexity is that many of the incidents in this book have more than one "correct" explanation. Two or even more of the alternatives may be helpful in explaining the incident. This is because there are often a number of factors to be considered before a conflict can be adequately explained. Sometimes the alternatives deal with different theoretical concepts that are useful in understanding what happened, for example, collectivism and ownership. Other times they present reasonable explanations, one of which comes more from a Chinese perspective, another from an American perspective. Sometimes one helpful alternative offers a deeply historical perspective, another a more modern perspective.

We began by writing incidents based on actual events that had involved one or more of the authors or people with whom they were acquainted. It was easy enough to come up with stories of cross-cultural experiences that had, at the time they happened, angered or saddened the individuals involved. Sometimes one of us was the observer of the conflict and may or may not have stepped in as a cultural informant to bring about peace. On other occasions one of us might have been the confidant of one or more of the participants. Some incidents grew out of experiences we had while still new to the other culture and about which we felt we had gained some perspective over time.

For example, one of us went to an informal party in a foreign student dormitory and took along a young, female Chinese friend who spoke very good English. At the party, the author was overcome by a headache, and since the young Chinese woman was having a good time and was not ready to leave, the author left her with a responsible young Swiss man to whom she had already introduced the girl and asked him to see that she was all right until she was ready to leave. The room became very warm, and they tired of dancing. The Swiss student suggested a walk. The Chinese student responded coldly that she thought it was time for her to leave, which she did without delay.

The next day the author had visits from both students. The Swiss man had no idea how he had offended the young Chinese woman, and he was very distressed at having done so, as he had liked her a great deal. The Chinese student, for her part, was outraged by the behavior of this otherwise respectable and likable young man. When the author explained to the Chinese woman that going for a walk to cool off was, by the Swiss student's Western European standards, considerably less intimate than dancing in a crowded room, and to the Swiss student that a stroll around the campus in the dark would have seriously compromised the Chinese woman's reputation, both parties were eager to meet and apologize to one another. This incident was not included in the collection because we had others that dealt with similar issues. Nevertheless, it can be used to demonstrate how many of the incidents were created.

In this instance, we would give all three characters pseudonyms, but otherwise simply tell the story more or less as it occurred. The incident would require trainees to advise the author's character on how to smooth over the problem between the two students. One alternative would give the Swiss student's perspective (which would be shared by most Americans) that a walk in the dark was harmless and logical. Another alternative would give the Chinese woman's perspective, which was that a walk in the dark with a man had special significance that would not be missed by anyone they happened to pass. Both of these alternative explanations would be helpful in understanding the incident. Other less helpful alternatives would be the attributions that the two individuals made about each other: the Chinese woman's attribution that this young man was awfully fresh, and the Swiss man's attribution that this woman overreacted to a perfectly harmless suggestion and was perhaps a little overtired and overheated. When the incident was brought to the group, suggestions might be made about ways to make the alternatives more useful, and theoretical concepts to be included in the discussion of each alternative would be considered.

Sometimes we were able to write an incident very easily, since someone had a vivid recollection of a cross-cultural clash, but we found the alternatives more difficult to write. Before moving to the United States in 1992 Mary and Wei-zhong Wang spent two years together at Nanjing University, living on the psychological border between the large foreign community of teachers, students, researchers, and consultants and the Chinese community of teachers, students, support staff, foreign affairs office personnel, and their families. While trying to come up with appropriate incidents for inclusion in this culture assimilator, they would often begin by saying something like "Remember how angry Mrs. Chao got when Linda Peterson told her she didn't need a contact teacher?"

From there they would re-create the incident. Then they would write the alternatives, one of which would include what Mrs. Chao had said to Wei-zhong to defend herself, and another would be what Linda Peterson had said to Mary to support her position. A third might be an explanation offered by Linda's husband. The ideal explanation would be a fourth, devised by Mary and Wei-zhong, that took both perspectives into account, along with historical and cultural issues that neither of the participants in the incident might have had in mind. The interesting part is that it often took two or three days of arguing and discussion for this fourth alternative to be created, and sometimes it could not be constructed until the entire Chinese culture assimilator work group had met and discussed it thoroughly. Even then, as a group, we might have come up with two quite different explanations that would be helpful in gaining insight into the cultural issues that might have been behind the conflict, or we might have rewritten the alternatives that included the principal characters' attributions about each other in such a way that the validity of both perspectives was highlighted. In some places in the explanations, we have indicated that a perspective or alternative explanation was offered by either an American or Chinese author. In most cases, however, because of the highly collaborative nature of the work, we judged it impractical to separate the Chinese point of view from the American. In other instances, the distinction was clear without being explicitly labeled with phrases such as "from the perspective of the Chinese" or "from the perspective of one of our American authors."

Often incidents were based on a composite of experiences, that is, one or more of us had found ourselves in the same awkward position a number of times. An example would be the incident entitled "The Dinner Invitation." The Americans in our group had all had experiences where plans with Chinese friends were canceled with what we perceived to be an insufficient, almost mysterious, lack of explanation. We felt that even gentle questioning made the Chinese friend uncomfortable, causing us to feel unsure of the status of the friendship. We decided that this was a common experience that affected relationships between Chinese and Americans and therefore necessitated an incident.

As we continued to work on creating new incidents, it became clear that there were several theoretical concepts that were essential to understanding the conflicts that took place between Americans and Chinese. Any explanation of the alternatives, we found, included one—

or more often, several—of these key theoretical concepts: individualism versus collectivism, *guanxi* (connections) and interpersonal obligations, hierarchies, gender relations, rules and regulations, work incentives, and attitudes about ownership. (These concepts are defined and discussed in depth in Part One). Subsumed under these broader categories are such important concepts as respect for authority, how to establish friendships and networks of business contacts, what contracts mean, and how to understand and deal with bureaucracies.

Later incidents were frequently written to illustrate an important concept that had not been adequately covered by a previous incident. As the number of completed incidents grew, we realized that some concepts had been covered very thoroughly, while others had not received adequate treatment. We decided, for example, that we did not have enough incidents covering various aspects of differences in reactions to particular types of work incentives. We then brainstormed concepts from the literature on work incentives in China and the United States as well as situations we knew of where workers' motivations or reactions to incentives had created confusion or ill will. We were then able to write a number of incidents focusing on various aspects of motivating workers to do their best.

Our discussions made something else clear. Because our group included both Chinese and Americans, we found that we were generating both incidents and alternatives from both perspectives. Therefore, while culture assimilators are usually unidirectional, training people from one culture to move into the other culture (e.g., Americans going to China), we felt that with a little tweaking, we could make these materials more broadly useful. We decided to go ahead and write the incidents, alternatives, and explanations so that they could be used by Chinese interacting in the United States as well as by Americans going to China, and we thought they could be especially useful in situations where Chinese and Americans were learning to work cooperatively in any context. Indeed, while there is still a slight bias toward Americans planning to have interactions with Chinese, some of these incidents have been used successfully and with minimal editing to train Chinese people working in joint ventures in China to interact with their American coworkers and bosses.

Originally, we arranged the incidents in ascending order of complexity, but we felt that trainers and trainees would probably prefer a bit more structured organization. At the same time, we felt that it would do trainees no good if we arranged the incidents according to theme, since instead of asking trainees to recognize the role guanxi or hierarchy was playing in an incident, we would be telling them to look for it, thus diminishing the value of the incidents in helping trainees recognize the manifestation of these concepts. In other words, we would be "giving the game away." We settled on arranging incidents around the settings in which they took place. For those who wish to consider incidents focused around a specific theme, an index of the incidents, arranged according to the concepts they illustrate, can be found on pages 235–36. As we said earlier, trainees need not feel compelled to follow any particular order in covering the incidents. Each incident stands alone as a separate and complete piece.

The Validation of the Incidents

Of approximately fifty incidents, the authors chose forty-four that best illustrated the situations and concepts most likely to puzzle and create problems for those involved in Sino-American cross-cultural encounters. These incidents were validated according to guidelines presented in previous publications (Fiedler, Mitchell, and Triandis; Cushner and Brislin). Basically, validation generally involves showing the incidents to experts (for these materials, forty-one people) who rate the accuracy of the various explanations for each incident. Only those incidents on which the experts agree are retained.

Individuals who were approached to help with validation of the incidents were (1) Americans who had spent at least one year living and working or studying in China or Taiwan and (2) Chinese who had spent at least one year doing the same in the United States or Canada. Most of the validators had far more than a year's experience with the other culture; many had a lifetime. They were also known by at least one of the researchers to be culturally sensitive, observant individuals with no particular grudge against either culture.

Validators were asked to read each incident and then rate the four or five alternatives that followed it. Their choices were as follows:

I am certain that this is correct

Very likely

Likely

Unlikely

Very unlikely

I am certain this is not correct

Answers were assigned a number value from 1, for "I am certain that this is correct," to 7, for "I am certain this is not correct." Though there were only six choices, there were seven possible values. This is because a value of 4 was assigned in cases where validators drew an X between "Likely" and "Unlikely," wrote "I don't know," or left a blank for one alternative. In other words, we tried to pressure our validators to choose whether an option was likely or unlikely, but in cases where they insisted that they could not decide, we took it into account when compiling our results.

The validation results indicated that forty-one incidents were clear, useful, and unambiguous. In the few cases where the validation sample disagreed with our predicted "contenders" for best explanations, the validation sample was taken to be correct.

Explanations for each incident were revised and clarified on the basis of the validation results. A number of the experts made specific comments on one or more incidents or alternatives, and we also took those comments into account as we revised the explanations. Julie Haiyan Chao joined the team of authors at this point. She was able to contribute a second Chinese voice to the explanations and to draw on her experience in Hong Kong.

Chinese and American Names and Titles

The problem of what to name the Chinese characters in these incidents became a sticky one. There are a number of romanizations in common use. Hyphenation, capitalization, and spacing are inconsistent. Personal idiosyncrasies and preferences as well as regional dialects can influence how people choose to write their names or even the name they choose to use as the "English" version of their name. In this section we explain how we approached the naming of the Chinese characters in these incidents.

For all characters who were meant to be mainland Chinese, we have used *hanyu pinyin*, since that is the form of romanization used there. For Chinese Americans, we have used the forms of romanization more common in North America. In general we have avoided the problem of dialect in naming by assuming that all mainland Chinese characters would be using the Mandarin version of their names.

Chinese names begin with the surname, or family name, which is almost always a single character,[§] but occasionally two (e.g., Ouyang, Wu'er), followed by the given name, which can be either one or two characters. The Chinese do not have middle names, as most Americans do. A two-character given name can be written as two separate words, both capitalized. More often, it is written as a single word or as a hyphenated word, with one or both syllables capitalized. For example, a girl whose name is pronounced *wu ai ling* could write her name as Wu Ailing, Wu Ai-ling, Wu Ai-Ling, or Wu Ai Ling. The last of these alternatives is more common in Hong Kong, but in general personal preference is the guiding principle. In these incidents we have been intentionally inconsistent with regard to the punctuation of Chinese names, because inconsistency is what Westerners will encounter.

We have attempted to use naming in a way that is consistent with the context and the relationships involved. This can be a little difficult with cross-cultural relationships, where a Westerner may make different assumptions about what the context implies than does a Chinese counterpart. Among Chinese the use of given names, and nicknames based on given names, is frequently limited to family members or friends who have known the person since childhood. It is more common for young girls to be called by their given names than for boys, and much more common for children than for adults. By the teen years most Chinese children will use their classmates' family names, rather than given names, as a familiar form of address, though by far the most common form of address is to use the full name. Calling someone by his or her given name implies that no matter how far that person has come in life, to the speaker he or she is still a sweet little child. Obviously, this is not very respectful and does little to foster understanding and trust. North Americans should avoid the temptation to call acquaintances by their first names, unless they are specifically invited to do so. Chinese people who come to the United States or Canada to study or work find that they are called by their given names, and eventually they come to understand that no disrespect is intended. In the meantime, however, they may feel very uncomfortable. Some Chinese, on the other hand, welcome the use of their first name because they know "that is how Americans do it." We have used Chinese given names in some incidents where we feel that the Chinese person in question, or the setting, is sufficiently Westernized.

[§] All characters are one syllable.

Nicknames are common in China, but are generally used only within a particular collective. Until Westerners become quite familiar with the individual and his or her collective, they will not be expected to use nicknames.

Chinese people prefer nicknames and titles that give an indication of the interlocutors' relative positions in the social hierarchy. They are comfortable using titles like Dr. Watts, Vice President Zhang, Mayor Li, and some that are rather awkward for North Americans, like Deputy Assistant Shu, Gatekeeper Liu, and Department Head Ding. Westerners who urge colleagues or subordinates to use their first names will often find themselves called Mr. Joshua or Teacher Melanie by people who don't feel comfortable with the level of informality and adjust by adding a title. Among colleagues, neighbors, villagers, or others who form a relatively close collective, a very common form of address is used to indicate relative age, and thus relative status. *Xiao*, or "little," followed by the surname, is used to indicate younger members of the collective, while *lao*, or "old," again followed by the surname, is a title of respect for older members, usually males. These terms imply affection and trust as well as respect.

Using the last name only, which sounds awkward and high schoolish to many Americans, is comfortable for many Chinese. Among friends and co-workers, use of the last name only is very common, as is that of the full name. Wu Ailing will probably be called Xiao Wu by her superiors and Wu or Wu Ailing by her same-age colleagues and most others. Americans tend to feel fairly comfortable using "Mr.," "Ms.," "Miss," or "Mrs." plus a surname. These titles are also comfortable for the Chinese, particularly when the person addressed is of equal or higher status and/or age compared with the speaker.

Somewhere along the line, most English-speaking Chinese end up with an English name. Sometimes a new English teacher who feels overwhelmed by the effort to remember sixty Chinese names and faces will give all of the students English names, some of which will stick. Sometimes students of English or employees in a joint venture will choose a name at random, a name they have heard and like, the name of someone they admire, or a name that sounds or means something like their Chinese name. For example, Wu Ailing might become Eileen Wu, and Zhou Xuedong (literally "snow cold") may call herself Winter Zhou. Other times an employer will demand an English name, especially if an employee must answer phones. We know one Chinese man who was given the English name of the fellow he was replacing at his Hong Kong firm "for simplicity's sake."

While some Chinese resist adopting an English name, many feel it is convenient to have one for a number of reasons. By adopting such names, Chinese visitors to the United States avoid the discomfort of being called by their first names. Also, they often feel that it makes their hosts more comfortable. Another reason that some Chinese who have frequent contact with non-Chinese speakers may choose an English name is that they know it may be very difficult for foreigners to pronounce their names. They may feel empathy for strangers who are struggling, or they may simply tire of hearing their names mispronounced. In Hong Kong the use of both English and Chinese given names is institutionalized, and the standard order reflects both the Chinese and the English way of ordering names: English given name followed by family name followed by Chinese given name, for example, Robert Lui Cheuk Kei.

In some incidents we have used English names for Chinese people, placing them in quotation marks to indicate that this is an unofficial name chosen in adulthood. In incidents that take place outside of greater China, we have sometimes reversed the regular order of the Chinese name, placing the given name first and the family name last, in keeping with Western conventions. All of these confusing variations are common when Chinese and Westerners interact.

It is also very common for Western visitors to China to be given Chinese names. Official documents most often use a transliteration of the English name, which can be very lengthy; we have seen examples consisting of as many as seven Chinese characters. Friends or coworkers will frequently choose to invent Chinese names for a new arrival from abroad. This is a sign that the non-Chinese coworker is being invited, to a limited degree, into the ingroup. These names tend to be more like real Chinese names than the officially assigned versions, with only two or three characters and an auspicious meaning. Often considerable energy goes into choosing just the right name. Chinese friends will find these names easier to use. They can also help distinguish between two people whose names are homophones to the Chinese, such as Cassie and Kathy. Having a "real" Chinese name is often very useful in breaking down barriers with those who are not used to interacting with foreigners, especially those who speak little or no English.

Part One

Concepts for Analyzing Cross-Cultural Conflicts between Chinese and Americans

Individualism and Collectivism

Do people behave according to their own desires and preferences, or do they behave according to the desires and preferences of groups to which they belong? The answer, of course, is "sometimes the first way, and sometimes the second way." But there are two cultural dimensions, individualism and collectivism, that explain that in some cultures behavior is more often influenced by individual preferences while in others group desires are given a higher priority. Individualism and collectivism are the most extensively studied dimensions of culture (Hofstede 1980; Triandis 1995b; Bhawuk 1998) that have important implications for intercultural interactions. In broad terms, the distinction refers to people and goals. Do people emphasize their own personally set goals, or do they integrate their goals with those of others? People in the United States are more likely to choose the first alternative, and this is an indication of individualism. People in China are more likely to choose the second alternative, and this is an indication of collectivism.

As argued throughout this book, these cultural distinctions become clear when studying specific examples or critical incidents. Assume that a fifty-year-old woman receives a job offer in a city a thousand miles away from her current residence. It is an excellent job, but accepting it would mean moving away from her seventy-five-year-old widowed mother. The mother is beginning to show signs of the normal aging process, but she has good friends where she currently lives and has no desire to move to another city. What will the daughter do? In an individualistic culture, the daughter is more likely to pursue her own goals and take the job in the other city. In a collectivistic culture, she is more likely to take into account her mother's goals and stay in the same city with her.

Four features of individualism and collectivism have been identified that are especially helpful in analyzing cultural misunderstandings when this broad dimension might be playing a part (Bhawuk). The first is people's sense of their own self. Individualists are more likely to see themselves as the basic unit of their self-image. Following this, they place emphasis on their own goals, experiences, and preferences. This is called an independent self-image (Markus and Kitayama 1991). Collectivists are more likely to view their participation in groups as the basic unit of their self-image. Following this, they place emphasis on their relations with others, such as family members, school and work colleagues, and adherents to the same set of religious beliefs. This is called an interdependent self-image.

The second feature focuses on self-goals and group goals, and this has been introduced in the discussion of the fifty-year-old woman and her seventy-five-year-old mother. Other implications of this feature can be seen in the workplace and in the classroom. All five of the authors of this book have experience with the relative ease of setting up cooperative work teams in collective cultures. Collectivists are more prepared to integrate the efforts of four or five people. Individualists often prefer to put forth their own efforts and to be judged on the basis of those personal efforts.

The third feature involves attitudes versus norms. Individualists are more likely to behave according to their own attitudes. Collectivists are more likely to be attentive to group norms. Young married couples are often asked the question, "How many children will you have?" (Triandis 1995b). Individualists will respond according to their own personal preferences, such as their views of a desirable family size. Collectivists are more likely to take into account the norms of their group, such as the wishes of parents, grandparents, and siblings.

The fourth feature deals with rational and relational reasons for decision making. Individualists are likely to focus on reasons they consider rational. At times, these rational reasons are summarized in contractual terms. Collectivists are more likely to focus on reasons involving relations with other people. For example, individualist businesspeople may not renew a contract with a supplier if they discover another that will sell equal-quality materials for a lower cost. Collectivists will be more likely to take into account their long-term relationship with a supplier when making a decision concerning the continuance of a business relationship. Teachers are often faced with this rational/relational distinction. For example, according to test scores, a student has earned a high B grade, just below an A. If the teacher and student have known each other a long time, perhaps through family connections, should this be taken into account when deciding the student's grade?

Guanxi/Interpersonal Obligations

The concept of *guanxi* grows directly out of the collectivist nature of Chinese society. *Guanxi*, generally translated as "connections" or "relations," is central to an understanding of Chinese relationships (Luo and Chen 1996; Fang 1999). The vast majority of incidents in this collection deal with some aspect of guanxi.

The importance of guanxi reflects the rational/relational feature of the individualism/collectivism dimension. In an individualistic culture, people's access to health care, education, suppliers of materials for manufacturing, jobs, the attention of government officials, virtually everything they need to do or get, is proscribed by laws. The laws, which continue to be written and rewritten, passed, revised, and overturned, all strive, ostensibly, to "level the playing field" so that no one group or person gains an unfair advantage over others. Wealth becomes the crucial advantage in an individualistic society; one gets the quality one can afford to pay for. In a collectivistic society, access to all the goods and services mentioned above depends on one's relationships with the people able to provide them. Success depends as much on having a well-connected family and having attended school with the right people as it does on hard work and initiative. A person can work very hard to get a new business off the ground, but if he or she has no guanxi with the people who grant the licenses or with suppliers of difficult-to-get products or raw materials, no amount of hard work will be sufficient. Wealth is important in a collectivist culture as well, but it cannot override close family connections or generations-old friendships.

There are two ways of acquiring guanxi. The first is passive, at least initially. As is characteristic of a collectivist society, Chinese people make a clear distinction between insiders and outsiders. With insiders, one has guanxi, and one can accomplish things with the help of those people. In other words, one is born into certain guanxi networks: the extended family, parents' work unit, citizens of a small town. One joins other groups and adds them to one's guanxi network as one grows. Former classmates, roommates, and sports teammates are part of an adult's network of guanxi. For a doctor, present and former patients; for a teacher, present and former students, colleagues, and supervisors; for a businessperson, present and former suppliers, clients, and even some competitors—all are part of the inside group that he or she can rely upon. Members of one's inside group may be called upon to introduce one to members of their collective to whom one needs access. A person may have to travel some distance along the guanxi networks to accomplish an important task. Your former soccer teammate's cousin's wife's brother's co-worker may be the only person who can introduce you to the official whose approval you need to open your business or to the doctor who can perform your father's life-saving operation.

The second method of acquiring guanxi is to do favors for people. A person might want to establish guanxi with someone outside his or her existing collectives. Let's suppose that a mechanic meets a respected doctor when a postal clerk inadvertently hands them each other's packages. Knowing that sometime, perhaps not for many years, but certainly sometime, he or someone in his closest circle of family and friends is going to become ill, the mechanic will attempt to establish and strengthen guanxi between himself and the doctor. He'll offer to fix her car or bicycle, washing machine, or any other machine he can think of to suggest. If she accepts, he then knows that sometime in the future he can go to her for help when he or a loved one needs medical care or a hospital bed.

It is this second method of establishing guanxi that frequently gets Westerners into trouble. Accepting favors, especially large, important favors, puts one in "guanxi debt" to the person who grants the favors. It can be difficult to tell, initially, whether someone is acting out of kindness or if that person has an agenda. It is generally advisable to return favors, in kind, as quickly as possible, to avoid building up guanxi debt that may be called in at a very inconvenient time. If a new acquaintance introduces you to a number of important people, or if an old acquaintance suddenly comes forward offering to take you on a trip or help you obtain something valuable, vigilance is advised.

It is important not to confuse guanxi with concepts more familiar to Western readers, such as "networking." Networking tends to be comparatively superficial and goal-oriented. Guanxi is forever. Twenty years after graduation, one can call upon a high school or college class-mate to mobilize his or her relatives to help solve a problem. Most Americans have, at most, two or three such relationships—friends going back to childhood, for whom one would do anything. Rarely do such friendships extend into a second or third generation. Certainly North Americans are unlikely to define themselves in terms of their network of friends and relatives. A North American's first response when faced with a difficult task or troubling problem is to think, "What can I do to accomplish what I need?" whereas the Chinese person's first response tends to be, "Who do I know that can help me accomplish this?" In establishing business relationships, Chinese business-people are also thinking about long-term, ongoing relationships. All types of relationships—friendships, business partnerships, or academic exchanges—take a relatively longer time to establish in China than in the United States, and once established they are not easily abandoned. The connections remain, even after long periods of time without contact or activity.

The obligations to those within the collective are arguably the most powerful obligations a Chinese person has. They override laws, previous commitments to people outside the collective, and, in some cases, "the greater good." When a Chinese person appears to a Westerner to be a "bad citizen" who is breaking the law without apparent remorse or is lying or cheating to gain something for a relative or a friend, it is often the case that the Chinese person is behaving in a way that would not be likely to bring censure among his or her own people. To help the members of one's collective to achieve important goals is generally honorable behavior, even if it conflicts with other types of obligations.

Take, for example, the student who wishes to study in the United States. His marks are very good but not, perhaps, good enough. His aunt, who works in the school printing office, will *la guanxi* (pull on her connections) with a former colleague who has been transferred to the records office and ask her to upgrade her nephew's grades on his transcripts. His father's boss will convince a professor, a former class-mate of his who taught the boy one course and does not even remember who he is, to write a glowing recommendation, far overstating his qualifications and performance. Other family members and friends will do everything they can to assist the boy in achieving his goal, certain that he will do well and bring them honor if only he can get his chance. Individuals outside the collective will criticize the length to which the family is going to achieve their goal, but if they were in the same situation, they would feel obligated to do the same. That they might be doing a worthy stranger out of a deserved chance to study is not of concern to them. The chance to help someone within the collective achieve an important goal far outweighs any possible perceived harm to a stranger. It is up to that stranger's collective to support him or her.

This is not a simple issue. The Chinese government's ambivalence about corruption led to the 1989 occupation of TianAnMen Square by students and workers. This sort of official corruption (Overholt 1993) is a large-scale version of the same type of relationship that exists between loyal extended family members or close-knit classmates. Doing favors for people with whom one has guanxi is expected, even honorable behavior. However, those outside the collective, who are competing for resources and access, are bound to see such favoritism as unfair. Also, Chinese people who are asked to perform ethically questionable acts for someone at the fringe of their collective may experience discomfort and feelings of guilt. They may feel forced to help. For example, the aunt's former colleague who is asked to change the transcripts in the example above may feel used and uncomfortable. On the other hand, she may feel happy that she is in a position to be useful to members of her collective that need her. In any case, the personal obligation takes precedence.

Hierarchies

Several types of interpersonal obligations explored in these pages involve individuals' relative positions in hierarchies. China has traditionally been a hierarchical society. Confucius' teachings emphasize obedience to authority, respect for one's elders and betters, and female deference to male superiority (Chinese Culture Connection 1987). In the past not only one's own attainments but also the accomplishments of one's ancestors conferred high status upon some members of society, while confirming the subservient status of others.

The Communist Revolution shattered certain types of hierarchies, such as those based on wealth or on the accomplishments of one's ancestors. At the same time, it created new hierarchies based on Communist Party membership, political power, and control of key industries and goods. The recently implemented economic policies are creating new hierarchies based on wealth and control of resources. Though it was seriously challenged during the Cultural Revolution, respect for elders is simply too deeply ingrained in the Chinese culture for it to have been overturned in ten, or even fifty, years. In any case, China has remained a country where one's position in society is important and relatively difficult to change.

Essentially, the Chinese are what Geert Hofstede (1980) called a high power-distance culture. They are most comfortable when relationships are vertical and clearly defined. While not nearly so rigidly hierarchical as the Japanese and Koreans, Chinese people are generally happier when they know who the high-status and the low-status people are in an interaction (Brislin and Hui 1993). Much is made of age, advanced degrees, and job titles, since these clarify hierarchical relationships. North Americans, on the other hand, find it easier to interact with each other when there is at least the illusion of equality among members of the group. Americans frequently express respect for a boss who is just one of the guys or for a colleague who has great wealth or a prestigious family background but who "acts just like the rest of us."

This difference between the Chinese and North Americans is reflected in the language each uses to address friends and colleagues. Americans move immediately to the use of first names in the vast majority of situations. In some areas of the United States children may call their teachers and principals by their first names. Colleagues in an office very rarely refer to each other by title or as "Mr." or "Ms." There are exceptions, however. Some individuals prefer the use of a title plus their last name. Both Ph.D.s and M.D.s are generally called "Doctor" in a professional environment, and the U.S. president is never publicly addressed with his first name. Chinese people are frequently called by their titles: doctor, teacher, professor, manager, boss, gatekeeper, and so on, followed by the surname. It is interesting that while the Communists attempted to eradicate class differences, in part by prohibiting the use of status-specific titles and replacing them with the all-purpose *tongzhi*, or "comrade," the status titles made an immediate comeback the moment restrictions were relaxed. Americans who try to get their students to call them by their first name will invariably find themselves addressed as "Teacher" by at least some of their students, those who do not feel comfortable addressing a teacher as an equal. Though many people who have frequent dealings with foreigners adjust easily, after a time, there are still those who feel quite uncomfortable having people who are not their intimates call them by their first names. Chinese most often express an affectionate but respectful relationship by adding *xiao*, or "little," to the surname of younger friends and colleagues and *lao*, or "old," to the surname of older colleagues.

Harry C. Triandis, Richard W. Brislin, and C. Harry Hui (1988) suggest that one of the most difficult cultural differences to overcome, for North Americans and others like them who are socialized to value egalitarianism, is this acceptance of, and even comfort with, status differences. Particularly in the workplace, high power distance can be unsettling to those from low power-distance cultures. The Chinese boss has an authority over workers' private and professional lives that most individualists find hard to tolerate (Dorfman 1996). The boss may offer unsolicited advice about personal matters and even suggest suitable marriage partners to subordinates. The Chinese boss expects such interference to be taken seriously and kindly. Most Chinese people in subordinate positions are happy to place their trust in their superiors. They tend to feel that those above them in the hierarchy are truly their superiors and are looking out for their welfare from a broader perspective and a greater base of experience than they could themselves. Status brings with it great responsibility to do what is best for one's subordinates. Those in positions of power are expected to use that power responsibly and to advance the interests of all those in their collective. As one example of the benefits lower-status members may enjoy, any serious error made in the workplace, for example one that involves a bad investment that costs the firm a great deal of money, will be "covered" by the boss. A superior takes responsibility for everything done by those under his or her authority.

Gender Relations in the Workplace

In the first half of the twentieth century, it was still common in China for women to set eyes on their husbands for the first time on their wedding night. Marriage was not, primarily, the union of two individuals; it was the union of two families (Fukuyama 1995). Whether or not the couple would love each other, or even get along, was not especially important. Much more important was that they produce sons to bring honor and wealth to the male's family. Courtship was virtually nonexistent. Women and men operated in very different spheres. Women were confined to the home. There is an archaic term for *wife* in Chinese that means "inside person," and, of course, most people know about foot-binding, which kept women from ever going very far from the home without a great deal of assistance. Men did not consult with women about anything of importance. Women existed to produce sons. Though there have been exceptions throughout Chinese history, and fairly frequent exceptions during the past century, it is wise to remember that for thousands of years, there were virtually no women at all in politics or business. It is not surprising, therefore, that the question of how women ought to be treated as co-workers is still a rather perplexing one in the Chinese workplace.

The Communist Revolution put an end to marriages arranged to ensure the continued concentration of wealth and power in the hands of a few families. However, Western ideals of romantic love still had little place in courtship and marriage. Even when couples were allowed to choose their own marriage partners, they tended to consider how best to improve their social status, political position, and, of course, guanxi, as they had been culturally conditioned to do. Compatibility, shared interests, and affection were of far less importance to most couples. Passion was reserved for politics. Husbands and wives were expected to endure long separations to do "The Work of The People." The same, of course, was true of courting couples. In addition, there was a strong element of prudery in Chinese Communism, in part a reaction against "decadent" behaviors that had infiltrated from the West in the late nineteenth and early twentieth centuries. These decadent behaviors included such things as kissing and dating more than one person before marriage. Only in the past two or three decades, with the economic reforms and the opening up of China increasingly to the West, have attitudes relaxed at all. It can be a mistake to think that too much has changed.

Playing the dating game in a foreign context is always complex (Cushner and Brislin 1996). North Americans doing business with the Chinese need to understand that the casual date, so familiar to Westerners, does not exist in China. One-on-one dating is serious business, and so simple an act as inviting an individual to go for a walk or join one for a cup of coffee may be fraught with implications. If sojourners wish to avoid finding themselves in the awkward position of trying to extricate themselves from an unintended engagement, under the censorious eyes of their co-workers, they would be wise to restrict socializing with the opposite sex to going out in groups. Singling one individual out from the group for particular attention is tantamount to announcing intentions to marry. It is not even necessary that the Westerner behave in a way that is flirtatious or romantic for his or her behavior to be misinterpreted. As we have attempted to make clear, courtship in China can be decidedly "undewy-eyed": practical, straightforward, and powerfully unromantic.

Before one thinks, "Oh, what can it hurt?" it is wise to remember that it is usually the Chinese person, who has to continue to function within the Chinese culture, who is likely to suffer the most. An unwanted transfer to another department, or even another city; a reprimand; actions that signal a lack of trust from co-workers; being passed over for promotion, training, or important projects; perhaps even public criticism—any or all may be the punishment for a Chinese person who becomes involved with, or even appears to possibly have become involved with, a foreign co-worker. Even today, dating more than one or two individuals before marriage is considered indicative of loose morals and a lack of dependability and stability, so a broken romance with a foreigner, even if only a perceived romance, can hurt a person's chances of a good marriage.

Finally, North Americans may be surprised to learn the extent to which "their own business" is everyone else's business, especially in the workplace. Supervisors may actively promote dating and marriage among their subordinates, but they are also quick to intervene when they see that relationships that they consider inappropriate are being formed. Nearly any romantic relationship between a Chinese and a foreigner will be considered inappropriate, at least initially, so a non-Chinese who gets seriously involved with a colleague should expect a lot of outside interference and unsolicited advice. A boss who does interfere is merely doing his or her job and can be considered to be acting appropriately in terms of his or her position in the hierarchy. The workplace is a collective, and its members must think about what is good for the collective. One way a good boss does this, proving a justified position in the hierarchy, is by making sure that subordinates are happy and secure in all aspects of their lives.

Rules and Regulations: Deference to Authority

Westerners visiting China have been known to become immensely frustrated by the expression "*You guiding*," meaning "There is a regulation." It seems that whenever one asks for the reasons behind a seemingly illogical refusal or request, one is told there is a regulation. A *guiding* is not, strictly speaking, a law, most of the time. If you ask to be shown a copy of the regulation in question, you may be told that there is a *guiding* forbidding showing the *guiding* to foreigners. There are many reasons why people, foreigners in particular, might not get an explanation for a change of plans or an inconvenient situation: someone may be trying to save face; there may not be a clear, simple explanation; or the person asking may not have adequate guanxi. Most often, though, someone in authority simply judges that the person asking has no particular need to know. In China, bureaucratic authority takes precedence over written rules and regulations.

As a general rule, Chinese people trust in those who make decisions for them (see "Hierarchies," page 34), and even if they don't trust them, they feel that it is beyond their power to change things. They are, therefore, less likely to question authority than are North Americans, and less likely to be troubled if situations are not explained to them (Bond 1986; Chinese Culture Connection). Also, because they are members of the culture, possible explanations may occur to them that make sense in the larger context, explanations that do not occur or even make sense to the foreign visitor, even if explained.

Work Incentives

There is a greater range of salary and benefit packages in China than exists in the United States. For example, a college graduate seeking employment in the United States can expect a reasonable salary plus benefits such as medical insurance, participation in a retirement plan, and sometimes dental care and access to child-care facilities. The salary should be large enough so that employees can provide housing for themselves. Good jobs will also have business travel opportunities. The range of benefits provided by these packages across organizations is relatively limited, and organizations have to constantly monitor these packages to compete for the best employees (C. J. Zhu 1999).

In China, the range in the salary and benefits packages that are offered to employees is much broader, especially given the categories of organizations that people know well and discuss among themselves: state-owned enterprises, joint ventures, private companies, family-run businesses, and hybrids of these. Beyond their salary, employees can expect various benefits that can act as incentives. Examples are a salary sufficient to cover housing, housing itself, participation in a retirement program, child care, medical insurance, and so forth. Commissions and bonuses for good work can also serve as incentives, but these are sometimes presented to individuals in a way that does not interfere with their membership in their collectives. For example, a boss might present bonuses in private rather than in a public forum. If the employer has good guanxi, access to these connections can also be a work incentive (Luo and Chen). For example, if a boss has a good relationship with a government official who has desirable resources to distribute, he or she might introduce a hard worker to this official. Travel is also an incentive. Chinese workers who perform well are sometimes sent on excursions labeled as "business trips" but where the focus is more on vacation than work. Trips outside China are highly valued. Travel among co-workers, without spouses and children, is often seen as desirable, since people can then have a good time without the restraints that spouses and children might impose.

One type of work incentive is especially interesting given traditional Chinese culture. Assume a young man works for a family-owned business. If the owner has daughters but no sons, the aspiring young man might be brought into the family by marrying one of the daughters. As a son-in-law, he might inherit the business. Our colleague Dr. Yadong Luo points out that this scenario increases in probability if the owner of the business values Chinese tradition and downplays modern outlooks on business management.

Ownership

Who owns what? What sorts of things can be owned? And under what conditions are owners obligated to share the things they claim as their own?

From an early age American children are encouraged to respect the property of others by not cutting across neighbors' lawns, not using other children's toys without asking first, and by using public property, like library books or city parks, responsibly. Often respect for public property is encouraged with such admonitions as "Treat it as if it were your own." Children are urged to respect possessions, their own and others. One of the first concepts and words many toddlers master is "Mine!" While we encourage young children to share their toys, we also assume that it is within the child's rights to choose to share or not share the objects the child owns. Things belong to individuals.

Collectivists like the Chinese differentiate far less between "mine" and "ours." Within the collective, there is very little that, strictly speaking, belongs to one person alone. With the members of the collective—the family, college roommates, co-workers, teammates—the collectivist shares wealth, knowledge, intimate thoughts, and access to powerful people as well as troubles and debts (Bond). As a result, from childhood the Chinese tend to be less possessive about objects. They may be annoyed when something they want is not available to them when they need it, but they will not blame the person who is using it.

Let's illustrate with an example. Eight young men share a dormitory room. Two of them have bicycles. If any one of the roommates has an errand to do, he will take one of the bikes. If the roommate who owns the bicycle is around, the borrower will tell him that he wants to use it, but otherwise he will just tell another roommate or friend to pass the message along. Suppose the owner of the bicycle comes back to the dorm from classes, intending to use his bike to get to an appointment across town. The bike is not there, so he has to take the bus or make some other arrangement that is certainly less convenient, and he may even miss his appointment. An American might ask the bike owner, "Weren't you angry that your roommate took your bike without asking permission?" to which the answer would probably be a baffled "Angry?". Members of a collective, like roommates who get along, don't need to ask permission to use each other's things. That his roommate needed it first is all the explanation the owner requires, in spite of any inconvenience to himself.

This is hard for many Americans to grasp. Imagine if your neighbor and very good friend took your car whenever he had a need for it. He always filled it with gas and took care of any repairs that were needed while the car was in his possession. He would tell you that he was taking it if you were home, but if you weren't, he would just use it. And it doesn't bother you at all.

Another aspect of the ownership issue is to question exactly what can be owned. The United States is a very legalistic society. We maintain the highest number of lawyers per capita in the world (Triandis 1995b) to help us keep track of who has the rights to what. One of us knows a lawyer who had the job of swooping down on retailers who were using Sesame Street characters in their advertising without first obtaining permission. Popular musicians have been forced to pay huge penalties for using a few bars of music from a relatively unknown song without giving proper credit to the original composer. Researchers lose their funding, graduate students lose fellowships, people can even lose their jobs or have advanced degrees taken away from them if they use the ideas of others without giving proper credit to the sources of those ideas.

In China, on the other hand, virtually anything that has been published or publicly performed belongs in the public domain. Consider Chinese history. For thousands of years all scholars studied for and passed the same examinations. Their studies involved reading and memorizing the classic, accepted works. Everyone who could read knew Confucius and Lao Tzu. Every scholar could recite the ancient poets. To cite the source of a quotation would be an insult to an educated listener or reader, as if to say "I am better versed in the classics than you are." The only time one would cite a source would be to instruct a pupil. More recently, Chairman Mao's *Little Red Book* and the writings of Lenin and Marx were widely studied. Again, anyone who could read would know the same works. There was simply no need to cite sources, and to do so was, again, an insult to the listener. The Western obsession with careful documentation of sources in academic writing, for example, no doubt seems very strange to the Chinese: unnecessary and disrespectful to one's readers.

If one thinks about it, the ownership of words and ideas is an odd concept. Just because someone writes something down and copyrights it does not mean that that person was the first to think those thoughts or say those words. So the right to ownership of text is not really an inalienable human right; rather, it is provided for by the laws of a country, usually an individualistic country. Confucius went so far as to condemn royalties and any other sorts of profits from written work. He taught that to profit from what one had written was destructive of group harmony, and since nothing was more important than group harmony, private ownership of texts and ideas was to be avoided.

Part Two

At Home

1 Too Close for Comfort

James had recently arrived in Nanjing for a study abroad semester. A graduate student in engineering, he wanted to increase his ability to speak and read Chinese. He hoped this would give him an edge in taking advantage of future opportunities in the growing Chinese economy.

He had already met his roommate, Wu Zemin, and several of the students in adjacent rooms. Most of them were studying engineering as well but had limited experience with Americans. James had learned Chinese back home in the United States, but he found that "real Chinese" was quite different from what he had learned in the classroom. That evening, James went with Wu Zemin and several other students to the cafeteria for dinner. After dinner James was ready to settle down for his first study session back in the room. Wu told James he was going next door, where one of the students had a small TV. They were going to watch World Cup soccer, and Wu asked James to join them. James told Wu he might come over after a while.

Later, James decided to see what the guys were up to next door. He found Wu and two of the three students who lived there huddled on bunks and chairs. James found it quite odd, however, that Wu was draped over the back of the student seated in front of him on a chair and was adjusting a few dials on the TV. Moreover, the student seated in front of the TV had his feet propped up on his roommate, who was seated nearby. It appeared to James that he had startled them, since they jumped up and welcomed him and even offered him tea. After James had a cup of tea and found a chair to sit on, the group returned to the match.

James shrugged the incident off, but over the next few days he noticed that female students on campus frequently walked arm in arm or even held hands. He noticed, too, that students of both sexes, but especially the males, would huddle around the newspaper displays outside the dormitory in a fashion that was similar to Wu Zemin and the others around the TV. James felt rather uncomfortable and wondered how he would respond if one of his classmates were to put his arm around him.

What's going on? Help James understand.

1. James is just going through culture shock and is overreacting to something that is not really that different.

2. James is too uptight in his relationships. He should loosen up so as to feel more comfortable.

3. Nanjing is considered one of the more progressive cities in China, and alternative lifestyles are readily accepted.

4. In Chinese culture close personal contact is more widely accepted than is such contact in James' culture.

5. James is too conservative in his moral philosophy. He should be more temperate toward the social behavior of other people.

Explanations for Too Close for Comfort begin on page 53.

2   Are You Mad at Me?

Charlie Turner was pleased to have been assigned an international student as his roommate in his sophomore year at the small Midwestern liberal arts college he was attending. Ji Bing was easygoing, a good listener, warmhearted, and always ready for a new experience. He appreciated Charlie's explanations of American culture and unfamiliar idioms and expressions. Charlie didn't think Ji Bing was any more difficult to get along with than the American roommate he had had the year before, except that he seemed to want to study more than Charlie was used to and he sometimes borrowed Charlie's things without asking first.

One night Charlie was working on a project that required a bit of artwork. Ji Bing was at his desk studying for a test. Charlie's scissors were just too dull to do the job, so he asked Ji Bing, "Sorry to bother you while you're studying, but could I use your scissors for a while?" Ji Bing said, "Sure." He opened his desk drawer and handed Charlie the scissors. "Thanks, thanks a lot," Charlie said. A few minutes later, Charlie decided that his markers were not going to do the trick, so he addressed his roommate again. "Sorry to bug you again, but these markers are too fat. You know those colored pencils you have? Would it be okay if I used them for my project?" Ji Bing got up, got them off the shelf, said, "Help yourself," and went back to reading as Charlie thanked him. After another few minutes, Charlie said, "I must be driving you crazy, but have you got any glue or tape? I promise I'll buy you another roll." Ji Bing handed Charlie a roll of tape that was on his desk, saying, "Use as much as you want. I don't need it." "Appreciate it," Charlie mumbled as he went back to his project.

Ji Bing went back to his reading. As Charlie was putting the finishing touches on his work, he noticed that Ji Bing was watching him. He looked up and was surprised to hear his Chinese roommate ask him in a plaintive tone, "Are you mad at me?"

"Of course not," Charlie replied, "what makes you think that?"

What culturally based misunderstanding has taken place between these roommates?

1. In China good friends do not generally use such polite language with each other, unless they are annoyed.

2. Ji Bing really meant, "I am mad at you." He was irritated by the frequent interruptions of his study for such trivial reasons. Chinese people frequently use this type of indirect, opposite-

meaning question to express irritation with others, much as an American might sarcastically say "Excu-u-use *me*" to someone who is being rude.

3.   Chinese people place a much higher value on learning than do Americans. It is considered extremely rude to interrupt a student who is engaged in studying. That Charlie interrupted Ji Bing three times in such a short period of time convinced Ji Bing that Charlie was deliberately annoying him and must have been angry.

4.   Ji Bing didn't understand why Charlie didn't just take the things he needed. Among Chinese roommates who are friendly with each other, there should be no need to ask permission to use items of such small value.

Explanations for Are You Mad at Me? begin on page 55.

3   What Is Dinner at a Friend's?

Janice Linzer was a young engineer working for a pump manufacturing joint-venture operation in Wuhan. She had studied Chinese for two years at college and felt her competency with Chinese was growing rapidly; she was even learning a little of the local dialect. She felt lucky that her husband, George Carter, had been willing and able to make the move with her and that he, too, seemed to be enjoying his English-teaching job and their new life in Wuhan.

Janice felt that she got along well professionally with her Chinese colleagues, but she wished she could get friendlier with them; they seemed a little distant and cautious. She was really pleased, therefore, when Liu Ling-ling, another engineer, who seemed slightly less shy than the rest, invited Janice and George to her home for dinner one Friday night after work.

Ling-ling met them at the bus stop and took them to her home, a sparsely furnished but very clean two-room apartment. She briefly introduced them to her husband, Yang Feng, who was busy in the tiny kitchen, and then invited Janice and George to sit down in a room where there was a table with eight plates of various cold dishes on it. She served them some tea and then disappeared for fifteen minutes. Just when Janice was about to get up and go ask if anything was wrong, Liu Ling-ling returned and added hot water to their tea. In answer to their offers, Liu Ling-ling assured them that she and her husband didn't need any help in the kitchen. She pointed out a new CD player that she and Yang Feng had recently purchased and their thirty-five-inch color TV and invited the American couple to have a look at them. Then she disappeared again. After nearly three quarters of an hour, Ling-ling reappeared. The three of them sat down and began to eat. Yang Feng came into the room from time to time to put hot dish after hot dish on the table. Most of the food was wonderful, but there was far too much of it. Janice passed on the eels and the sea cucumber, and George skipped the one-hundred-year-old eggs and the fatty pork in pepper sauce. Both George and Janice were full before half the dishes had been served. Also, they couldn't help wishing that Yang Feng would sit down, so that they could get a chance to talk to him. When he finally did come in from the kitchen, he ate a bit and then turned on the TV, fiddling with the knobs to show them all of the features. Ling-ling next proceeded to demonstrate the CD player, and then it was late and time to go home.

Although they felt vaguely depressed by their first social encounter with Liu Ling-ling and Yang Feng, they felt that they should return the dinner invitation, so they invited the Chinese couple over two weeks later. George and Janice decided to introduce their new friends to an American meal. George scoured the hotels and grocery stores that catered to Western tastes. He was excited to find some black olives, tomato juice, soda crackers, and even some tolerable cheese. They set these out as appetizers along with some Chinese peanuts and small crackers. Janice made spaghetti and a salad. She even concocted some salad dressing from oil, vinegar, and some sweet-smelling but unidentified herbs she found at the market. George and Janice were pleased with their efforts. When Liu Ling-ling and Yang Feng arrived, they were obviously impressed by the apartment. They asked the price of the square of carpet, the CD/tape player, the TV, and the vacuum cleaner. They pressed every button on every appliance, and Janice was glad the food processor was tucked away in a kitchen cupboard. They nibbled without enthusiasm at the appetizers, but Janice was pleased that they seemed to be having fun. She did, however, refuse politely to answer their persistent questions about the cost of everything.

The Chinese couple seemed a little confused when both Janice and George sat down to the meal, and Liu Ling-ling asked who was doing the cooking. She still looked confused, even after Janice and George had explained who had prepared what. The two Chinese ate just a tiny bit of spaghetti and didn't finish the salad on their plates. George urged them to eat more, but they continued to refuse and to look around expectantly. George and Janice explained the origin of each of the foods served, found out where Liu Ling-ling's and Yang Feng's families were from, and learned quite a bit about Yang Feng's job as a physics professor. They also answered questions about their own families and hometowns. When it seemed everyone was done eating, George cleared the table and Janice served coffee and some chocolate pastries she had found in a hotel bakery. Liu Ling-ling put four spoonfuls of sugar in her coffee and drank about a third of it. Yang Feng took one sip and left the rest. Neither ate more than two bites of pastry.

After they had left, George said to Janice, "At least we had a chance to talk," but Janice replied in a dismayed voice, "We left their place so full we couldn't walk, but they're going to have to eat again when they get home. What went wrong?"

As a friend of George and Janice's, how would you explain to them what cultural assumptions were at work that kept them from having a successful dinner party with their new friends?

1. Chinese people just don't like American food. George and Janice should have attempted to cook Chinese food, which their guests would have been more accustomed to eating. This would have made Liu Ling-ling and Yang Feng feel more at ease.

2. While discussions of money and prices embarrass Americans, they are quite normal for Chinese. Yang Feng and Liu Ling-ling sensed that George and Janice felt awkward and unhappy with the discussion before dinner, and as a consequence *they* felt awkward during the meal. That's why they didn't eat much.

3. For Americans, conversation is more important than the food itself, while for Chinese, the quantity and quality of the food is of primary importance at a dinner party; the conversation is considered quite unimportant.

4. Liu Ling-ling and Yang Feng were disappointed that Janice and George did not show them the household appliances and equipment, which were excitingly high-tech to them. Then, they were made even more uncomfortable by being asked personal questions about their families and jobs. They showed their unhappiness with the conversation in a traditionally Chinese way, by refusing the food offered by their hosts.

5. These two couples just don't have very much in common. Liu Ling-ling and Yang Feng are interested in material possessions and high-tech equipment, while Janice and George are more interested in people.

Explanations for What Is Dinner at a Friend's? begin on page 57.

4   You Can Afford It

Penny had spent two years teaching English in China seven years earlier and was very happy to be back in the country. In a few months she had brushed up on her Chinese and become used to the many changes that had taken place since she had left. Just as in her first job years ago, she was getting along well with her colleagues and students.

The city where she was now teaching was not far from the smaller town where her first teaching assignment had been. Quite a few of her students from that first teaching job were here in the city working or in graduate school. It was really nice for Penny to feel as if she had old friends as well as new ones around her.

One former student who occasionally came to visit Penny was Huang Zhi-qing, who had been working in a government office for the six years since his graduation. Huang Zhi-qing was a quiet young man, but he seemed comfortable chatting with Penny about his job, their old times together when he was a student, former classmates he had seen or heard from, or current events. He was especially eager to discuss his plans to go to graduate school abroad. He often asked for Penny's advice about his preparations for the GRE and his applications to American schools, advice she was happy to give. She had spent several evenings writing letters of recommendation for him and was hopeful that he would get into a good graduate program.

One day when Huang Zhi-qing showed up to visit Penny, there was obviously something on his mind. His responses to Penny's attempts to make small talk were awkward, so she finally asked him what was on his mind. Huang Zhi-qing told her that he had been accepted into graduate school at the University of Wisconsin. When she congratulated him, he admitted that there was a small problem, but he was sure that Penny could help him. Penny assured him that she would be happy to help in any way she could.

Huang Zhi-qing explained that he had been granted admission and a tuition waiver, but he would not be eligible for a graduate assistantship until his second semester. His family had saved some money but not quite enough to cover all of his expenses. Huang Zhi-qing had heard that many Chinese work their way through school in the United States, illegally if necessary, and he was sure that he could do the same. However, in order to get a student visa he would need a sponsor, a U.S. citizen, who could guarantee that he would not become a financial burden to the state.

Penny apologized that she couldn't help, explaining that she just didn't have the kind of money to guarantee that she could pay Huang's expenses. Huang claimed he had an uncle who could lend him the money for a couple of months, long enough to transfer it to Penny's account in the United States, have the bank draft a letter saying that she had sufficient funds, and then transfer the money back to him. Penny objected, saying that even if she felt that was moral, which she didn't, she still couldn't afford to sign a contract that would hold her financially responsible for Huang for three years. Huang Zhi-qing insisted that Penny would never have to pay out, just sign a form saying that she would. When she persisted in claiming that she couldn't afford to take on that kind of responsibility, Huang Zhi-qing suggested that maybe Penny's parents would be willing to sponsor him. Penny was taken aback and told him that she couldn't possibly ask her parents to put up that kind of money for someone they didn't even know.

The conversation dragged on for over an hour, with Huang Zhi-qing insisting that all she had to do was sign a piece of paper and that Penny could trust him to never really ask her for the money, while Penny insisted that though she trusted Huang, the U.S. government would still expect her to cover his debts if he should get into trouble. At last, Huang Zhi-qing left. Penny felt bad about the encounter and was not too surprised that Huang Zhi-qing's visits to her apartment stopped. When they happened to see one another at a large gathering, they avoided each other.

What culturally based explanation can you offer for this unhappy and unsuccessful encounter?

1. In Huang Zhi-qing's culture but not in Penny's, the obligations of a teacher extend beyond the classroom and the period of instruction to things like financial sponsorship of former students.

2. In Huang Zhi-qing's culture but not in Penny's, signing a contract is something to be taken seriously, but not too seriously.

3. By the standards of his own Chinese culture, Huang Zhi-qing was making a huge imposition on Penny's friendship. He should not have approached her; he was simply desperate not to lose his chance to further his studies in the U.S.

4. Huang Zhi-qing saw his and Penny's relationship as more than a friendship. He asked Penny to sponsor his studies in the U.S. as an indirect way of finding out whether she was willing to

become serious about their relationship. Penny took his request for sponsorship at face value and misunderstood his real intent.

5. Penny realized that Huang Zhi-qing was unrealistic to think that he could work his way through school. She was fairly certain that she would get stuck with his debts, and she simply could not afford it.

Explanations for You Can Afford It begin on page 60.

Explanations for the Incidents in Part Two

1 Too Close for Comfort

1. This is not a very good answer. Culture shock is the emotional reaction of people when they experience overwhelming stress in a different culture. James does not appear to be overwhelmed in this incident, but he is curious and uncomfortable about a perceived cultural difference. The behavior is different enough from what James has come to expect that it is causing him anxiety. What makes one foreign visitor anxious will not necessarily bother someone else, but that does not mean that James' anxiety is an overreaction.

2. This is not a good explanation. The fact that James "shrugged off" the initial incident with his roommate and the others around the TV suggests that he is really quite open-minded. When people interact with individuals from other cultures, they naturally experience differences and encounter challenges to their worldviews. It is natural for James to feel uncomfortable when he sees Chinese male students behaving in a way that would be considered inappropriately intimate in his own culture.

3. This is a groundless argument. Nanjing is just another big city in China. The lifestyle there is not significantly different from that in other big cities. In any case, alternative lifestyles have nothing to do with this discussion. Wu Zemin's and his friends' behavior here as well as the female students' is decidedly "mainstream."

4. This is the best explanation. Spatial orientation is a distinguishing feature of culture and a source of much misunderstanding. In North America, for example, when two people meet each other at an informal gathering, they are comfortable with about three feet of space between them (Hall 1966). Closer distances may readily cause discomfort in one or both of the individuals. If the two are close friends, they may hug, in a brief frontal embrace, but they will rapidly move apart and maintain that three-foot distance.

   Close physical contact between members of the same sex is more widely accepted in Chinese culture than in American culture. The following reasons might explain such a difference. First, for more than five thousand years, China was a very masculine society. There were very clear definitions of the roles males and females should play and, thus, very clearly defined spheres of action. As a result, males and females spent a great deal of time in the company of *only* members of the same sex; in other words, there were more interactions among same-gender groups.

Second, in China, body contact such as patting another person on the shoulder is considered to be a very important way of expressing concern, trust, or intimacy. Such contact is expected in certain relationships, say, between roommates or classmates or co-workers, and if absent may indicate problems. Within one's ingroup, members of the same sex (but girls especially) sit on each other's laps, caress, play with each other's hair, and spend the night together in narrow twin bunks. However, the frontal embrace, or hug, with which many Americans feel comfortable is considered too intimate. Most touching is side to side (e.g., arm in arm or sharing a chair) or front to back (people leaning over others, as James observed at the newspaper display and in his neighbor's room).

A third reason might simply be crowding. Six or eight Chinese students generally share a room that Americans would think fit for two. Multigenerational families of six and seven share two-room apartments. Comfort with less personal space may simply be an adaptation to inevitable crowding. It's wise not to make too much of this explanation, however, since adaptations to overpopulation vary according to culture and socialization. For example, Japanese reactions to crowding are quite different from those of the Chinese.

Finally, homosexuality is unacknowledged in China. It is considered a disease or criminal behavior. Therefore, two men or two women touching in public would never be assumed to be sexually intimate. James' cultural conditioning leads him to read more into the contact than is really there.

Westerners in China may also notice that when high-ranking people are introduced to others, they tend to shake hands for a very long time, perhaps clapping the second hand over the shaking hand, intending to convey warmth and sincerity. This can be very uncomfortable for Westerners, who are accustomed to a firm but fleeting handshake.

5. This is not a good answer. Cultural differences exist no matter how conservative or how liberal people are. Although the degree of difference might vary because of individual perception, nationality, ethnicity, history, or personal experience, the cultural differences are there. There is no indication that James is making any moral judgments at all. He is uncomfortable because he is misinterpreting the behavior he is observing. Find an alternative that takes that into consideration.

2   Are You Mad at Me?

1. This is a reasonable answer. Among Chinese students who are classmates, roommates, or close friends, too many "pleases," "thank-yous," and "I'm sorrys" will be interpreted as sarcasm or coldness. In warm, comfortable, close Chinese relationships, these words that Americans rely on to make life cordial are characteristically missing. Charlie's attempts to apologize for interrupting Ji Bing's study may have seemed too formal to Ji Bing. This is only a partial explanation, however. Look for another good alternative.

2. While many Chinese do have a gift for sarcasm, it is unlikely that Ji Bing was demonstrating it here. The plaintive tone of his question did not suggest irony. He was probably more puzzled than irritated that Charlie continued interrupting him over these trivial matters rather than just taking what he needed.

3. An unlikely explanation. Chinese students, like those in many Asian countries, work very hard to get into university, either in their own country or abroad. The college entrance examinations are extremely competitive, as are scholarships to study in foreign universities. Even so, there is no special cultural stigma attached to interrupting a roommate who is studying. Individual Chinese students, like American individuals, vary in their ability to concentrate when there are interruptions, noise, or other activity in the room. It is not the interruptions themselves that bothered Ji Bing, but their nature. Look for a better explanation.

4. This is the best answer. The Chinese word *jianwai* (consider myself as an outsider) describes the situation perfectly. People often realize that they are being excluded from the ingroup if a counterpart is being exceptionally polite to them (Cushner and Brislin 1996). Charlie's behavior of continuing to ask permission for small items was interpreted by Ji Bing as jianwai.

Remember that Charlie had noticed that Ji Bing sometimes borrowed his things without asking first, though he found Ji Bing to be kind and thoughtful otherwise. Charlie, like many Americans, has been raised to respect other people's private property and not to take for granted his right to someone else's belongings. Among the Chinese, ideas of personal property and one's rights to it differ. There is a greater tendency to take for granted that one's close friends or relatives would want one to use what one needed rather than waste time looking for it or money buying it. By *asking* to use such insignificant items as tape, colored pencils, and scissors, which cost Ji Bing virtually nothing to lend, Charlie introduced a level of formality into the relationship that made Ji Bing uncomfortable. It also might have suggested to Ji Bing that Charlie, for some reason, thought he was stingy.

American students are frequently very annoyed by the seemingly cavalier attitude their Chinese roommates and friends take toward their possessions, particularly relatively delicate and expensive items like CD players, tennis racquets, or musical instruments. Unknowingly, however, the Americans often invite such "invasions of their property" by insisting on what appears to the Chinese to be an extremely casual relationship. By rushing the use of first names and nicknames, treating new friends to dinner in a restaurant, and so on, Americans establish an intimacy that implies, to the Chinese, a set of rights and obligations that the American does not understand or share. In China, friendships generally form more slowly than they do between North Americans, but once formed, the bond is strong (Gao and Ting-Toomey 1998; Y. Zhu 1999). Friends are not only people you know well and spend time with but also people you can trust and with whom you share your wealth and your intimate thoughts. The difference in ground rules for what constitutes a comfortably familiar yet respectful distance consistently causes problems between Chinese and American roommates.

3   What Is Dinner at a Friend's?

1. This is quite a reasonable answer, but it is not the best one. Chinese people, especially those who have had little reason in the past to become familiar with Western traditions, may find American food very strange. In China, being fussy about food is not necessarily considered as negative and childish as it may be in the United States. While consumption of Western food is becoming increasingly fashionable, and the explosion of American fast-food restaurants like McDonald's and Kentucky Fried Chicken is phenomenal, many Chinese still find American food repulsive and are unable to get used to eating it. It is particularly likely that coffee, which has a very different flavor from the green tea most Chinese drink, and the pastries, which would be much sweeter than anything Chinese people are accustomed to eating, would have been too much for them. Even so, the taste of the food was not the main problem here. Furthermore, it's quite unreasonable to expect Janice and George to try to cook Chinese food; their amateur efforts might well have generated even more unhappiness with the meal.

2. It is quite true that Chinese and Americans may hold very different ideas about what constitutes an appropriate topic for conversation, especially regarding money matters. Americans are frequently embarrassed when Chinese ask frankly what their salaries are and how much their possessions, especially expensive ones, cost. Americans simply do not discuss their finances in this way. However, there is no indication that Yang Feng and Liu Ling-ling sensed George and Janice's discomfort with the topic. Indeed, it seems that Janice was more bemused than offended by the predinner conversation. Also, there is no cultural reason why embarrassment about the conversation would result in the Chinese couple's refusal to eat very much. There must be another reason for their lack of appetite.

It is interesting to note that what is a perfectly appropriate, even a "safe" topic of conversation in one culture can be shockingly rude in another. One of the American authors has watched countless awkward incidents where well-meaning elderly American tourists asked high school or college students, "Do you have a boyfriend?" The student replies by blushing and cringing and then asserting, "Certainly not." Of course, people this age do have boyfriends and girlfriends, but it is not a topic of discussion with relative strangers. This question is perhaps comparable to asking casually of an American youngster of the same age, "Do you sleep around?"

3. This is the best answer. While both couples were sincerely trying to show the other their warmest hospitality, the message did not get through because of culturally conditioned differences in expectations. Janice and George felt abandoned when Liu Ling-ling and Yang Feng disappeared into the kitchen and left them alone. Their culture had conditioned them to expect that at least one of their hosts would remain with them and engage them in conversation throughout the evening (Triandis, Brislin, and Hui 1988). When their hosts did appear, the focus was not on developing a relationship between the two couples but on the food and the things in the room. The meal itself seemed excessive to Janice and George. It is more usual, in the United States, to cook just a little more than the people present are likely to consume. Many Americans are bothered by wasted food. The Americans were unable to appreciate the generosity of spirit that was meant to be conveyed by the abundant offerings of food.

    Liu Ling-ling and Yang Feng were enthusiastic guests, by their own standards, in the Americans' home. They admired the costly, modern possessions of their hosts and paced themselves admirably by just nibbling on the hors d'oeuvres. According to their cultural expectations, they assumed there would be numerous and varied dishes served. They also expected that one or even both hosts would be hard at work in the kitchen until nearly the end of the meal, producing one delicious dish after another. This explains why Liu Ling-ling and Yang Feng were confused when both Janice and George sat down at the table and why they looked around expectantly and ate so little. They were confused; they wondered who was doing the cooking, and they ate little because they expected more to be coming at any moment. George and Janice must have seemed stingy and inhospitable to them. The food and drink is of great importance at a Chinese dinner party, and the quality of such is a good indicator of the guests' importance (Brislin and Hui 1993). The more expensive the liquors, the more important the guests. Inadequate or poor-quality food and drink can cause offense, as the guests feel they are being told they are insignificant and unworthy of serious recognition. If there is not enough food and drink, guests will get the impression that the host doesn't take the dinner—and them—seriously and did not bother to be well prepared. Nevertheless, Liu Ling-ling and Yang Feng kept up the conversation to the end, and even tried to eat the pastries, which must have been much too sweet for them, since dessert in a Chinese home—if it is served at all—is usually a piece of fruit with tea, or perhaps a piece of hard candy.

A suggestion from one of our validators is that George and Janice could invite Liu Ling-ling and Yang Feng to dinner in a Western restaurant or at a hotel for foreigners. Such an invitation would establish the American couple's generosity and would be a treat that Liu and Yang would never be able to arrange for themselves.

4. This alternative is only partly correct. Many Chinese are very excited about the modern labor-saving appliances and high-tech entertainment equipment that are fast becoming available in their country. Liu Ling-ling and Yang Feng may have felt a bit of disappointment that George and Janice did not share their enthusiasm. The American couple, however, *did* let the Chinese look over their things quite thoroughly, more thoroughly than many with their cultural background might have felt comfortable doing. On the other hand, there is no reason to assume that Liu Ling-ling and Yang Feng were unhappy about being asked relatively personal questions about their families and jobs. George indicated at the end of the incident that he thought the conversation had gone quite well. In fact, exchanging information about your family

members, your work, and your hometown is appropriate conversational topics among people who are getting to know
each other in both cultures. Finally, the Chinese have no
tradition of refusing food from a host who provides them
with less than satisfactory conversation. Try again.

5. There is little evidence to support this answer. Janice and
    George must have had a fairly strong interest in the same
    kind of possessions that interested Liu Ling-ling and Yang
    Feng, since they owned them, and indeed had gone to the
    trouble of bringing them from the United States or some
    major Chinese city to Wuhan. The difference is that in Chi-
    nese culture, such possessions and their functions, prices,
    and qualities are considered more suitable conversation be-
    tween people who do not know each other very well than
    they are in American culture. That Liu Ling-ling has ven-
    tured to attempt to become friends with an American col-
    league showed that she must have been not only interested
    in people but quite courageous. In an environment where
    people are relatively unfamiliar with foreigners, she could
    have brought suspicion upon herself and her husband. These
    couples may learn to get along quite well if they can learn
    about the expectations they have and the differences and
    similarities between their two cultures and discuss them.

4 You Can Afford It

1. In China the student-teacher relationship is a permanent one.
    In addition the responsibilities of the teacher to the students
    extend beyond academic matters to personal affairs. Teach-
    ers may feel they have the right and/or obligation to intro-
    duce former students to potential marriage partners or give
    them unasked-for advice about jobs they are considering
    (Brislin 2000; Dorfman 1996). Since Penny showed so much
    interest in Huang Zhi-qing's efforts to get into graduate
    school in the United States, and since he assumed that it was
    no financial burden to her, he may have thought it reason-
    able to expect her to go this one step further to help him
    realize his academic ambitions. However, even the most
    dutiful former teacher would not be expected by anyone to
    put herself or himself in danger of bankruptcy for a former

student. While a teacher does have extended responsibilities to former students, serious financial commitment would not usually be one of them.

Notice that Huang Zhi-qing also suggested that Penny might turn to her parents. This suggests that, indeed, Huang Zhi-qing did not understand the different roles and obligations that authority figures/caregivers have in U.S. culture. One suggested way out of this situation would have been for Penny to agree to write to her parents about the matter, but also encourage him to seek out other possible solutions. In the future when Huang asked her about it, she could have claimed that she had not heard back from her parents (which of course she wouldn't have, since she never asked them). This would have allowed both Penny and Huang Zhi-qing to save face and maintain their cordial relationship.

This answer, then, provides part of the explanation. Look for a better answer.

2.   This is the best answer. In China, a contract is typically more a sign of good faith between two parties than a legally binding document (Overholt 1993). If a person who has signed a contract is unable to fulfill it, the other party will often overlook it, or at least renegotiate to allow for more time or easier terms. It probably didn't even occur to Huang Zhi-qing that anyone would seriously expect Penny to pay. He could not have imagined that the very thought of signing a contract that could make her legally liable for tens of thousands of dollars that she didn't have probably made Penny feel queasy. For Penny, such a contract would be a weighty obligation, a fact that Huang Zhi-qing's experience with contracts did not prepare him to understand. To Huang Zhi-qing, this request differed little from the previous requests he had made, like asking for letters of recommendation, which Penny gladly provided out of friendship.

One of our Chinese authors adds that in China, although signing a contract is serious, the contract itself should not be taken too seriously. Usually foreigners tend to do business with the Chinese strictly according to contracts. They may not succeed in their business ventures simply because their contractual mindset hurts their Chinese counterpart's feelings. The Chinese perceive contracts as part of bureaucratic formalities and subject to change if the need arises.

Although this is the best explanation, it is not the entire story. Look for another good answer.

3. While the imposition was indeed a large one, as Huang Zhi-qing's discomfort in bringing up the subject attested, the groundwork had been laid for him to make such a request of Penny. She had been very supportive of his efforts to go abroad. Also, while Huang Zhi-qing might have been able to understand that another Chinese person would be unable to make such a financial commitment, he would probably have found it difficult to imagine that Penny could not afford it. It is very hard for many Chinese to believe that not all foreigners are rich. Because they see foreigners spending more money than they can imagine on silk shirts and nice meals, they think that there is no end to the money. They sometimes can't appreciate the difference between someone who has one thousand dollars in the bank and someone who has fifty thousand. Huang Zhi-qing probably just didn't believe that Penny didn't have enough money to back him, so he kept searching for a way to persuade her of the importance to him of her agreeing to sign the contract. He was probably desperate not to let this chance at further education slip away, but that was not the main reason for his persistence. Look for a better answer.

4. This is not a good explanation. Penny was right to take his request at face value. In fact, such requests are alarmingly common. Visiting professors have told us that they were inundated with requests to sponsor colleagues' children and their own students, even within just a month of two of their arrival in China. There is no indication in the incident that Huang Zhi-qing had a romantic interest in Penny or vice versa. Their relationship had been strictly within the bounds of a proper Chinese former-teacher/former-student relationship.

5. Possibly true, but this is not the best answer. Penny had lived in China long enough to have heard plenty of stories about Chinese students who left for other countries, includ-

ing the United States, with a single suitcase and no financial support and who subsequently finished their Ph.D.s. The ability of the Chinese to endure hardship to get what they want is legendary. Penny certainly may have feared that she would get stuck with Huang Zhi-qing's debts if he was involved in an accident, got into trouble with the law (possibly for working illegally), or fell ill and could not work. However, there are deeper cultural issues here. Look for an answer that captures them.

Part Three

Traveling

5   Where's the Bus?

It was National Day and everyone had a long weekend, so the Foreign Affairs Office of a large university in Jiangsu Province had arranged a trip for its foreign teachers to the beautiful city of Hangzhou. Almost all of the foreign teachers decided to go. They were accompanied by a number of mostly monolingual Chinese-speaking guides from the Foreign Affairs Office along with some young teachers from the English, German, French, and Russian faculties to act as interpreters. Altogether, two busloads of teachers, students, guides, interpreters, and Foreign Affairs Office staff went on the trip. When they got to Hangzhou, they were unloaded at a hotel on the outskirts of the city, given a nice dinner, and told to meet in the lobby at eight o'clock the next morning.

In the morning, when they were ready to set off sightseeing, the teachers were told that they would have to take the city bus. They didn't understand why they should take the crowded, dirty, city bus when they had two comfortable touring buses, with drivers, in which they had driven to Hangzhou.

In fact, the Foreign Affairs Office had found out only after they got to Hangzhou that the city had passed an Emergency Traffic Control Regulation prohibiting buses without Hangzhou licenses from entering the city for the few days before, during, and after the holiday. The interpreters were told *not* to pass this information on to the foreigners, since non-Chinese "wouldn't be able to understand the reasons" for it. The interpreters were instructed simply to insist that the teachers take the city bus and, if necessary, to make up a reason.

The foreign teachers demanded an explanation from their interpreters, who tried to explain that they hadn't made the decision and didn't know the reason. When they could get no real answer, the foreigners resigned themselves to taking the city bus. The interpreters, who were also friends and colleagues, could see that not knowing what was going on was affecting their foreign friends' enjoyment of the trip, so one by one they leaked the reason to the foreign teachers. The teachers were then annoyed with the Foreign Affairs Office staff for trying to deceive them. "Why couldn't they have just told us the truth in the first place?" they asked. The Foreign Affairs Office was annoyed with the interpreters for not following directions and blamed the interpreters for the fact that the foreigners were annoyed. By evening, everyone was irritated with someone, and the holiday was turning out to be no fun at all.

How might you explain to the foreign teachers and to the Foreign Affairs Office staff why this misunderstanding occurred?

1. The Foreign Affairs Office staff were embarrassed that they hadn't planned more carefully. They were afraid that they would get in trouble if word got back to their superiors that they had ruined the trip, so they bluffed and tried to pretend that the plan was to take the city bus all along. The foreign teachers should have gone along with the bluff to help the staff save face.

2. The Foreign Affairs Office mistakenly believed that the foreign teachers would blame them for this inconvenience. They were also ashamed by the backwardness of their country, which created this problem. They were concerned with maintaining face, which was reasonable in this situation, given their cultural conditioning.

3. The foreign teachers, who had been culturally conditioned to expect a reasonable explanation for problems, were angered by what to them were transparent lies about the cause of a change of plans. The Foreign Affairs Office would have best minimized loss of face if they had explained the real reason for the inconvenience and apologized.

4. The Foreign Affairs Office had blundered by providing interpreters from the ranks of the foreign teachers' colleagues. Since the interpreters were friends of the foreign teachers as well as employees of the Foreign Affairs Office, their loyalties were

divided. The Foreign Affairs Office should have tried to use interpreters who were strangers to the teachers and could thus have presented a united front, without conflict.

5. Telling a lie is not considered immoral in China, as it is in the West. By instructing the interpreters to lie, the Foreign Affairs Office staff did not feel they were doing anything wrong.

Explanations for Where's the Bus? begin on page 77.

6   Off on Her Own

A group of foreign teachers are on a sight-seeing trip arranged by the Foreign Affairs Office of their university. The itinerary includes a visit to a temple. The bus drops the group off at one entrance of the temple gardens and drives to the other side, where it will wait for them. The plan is for the group to climb the two hundred steps to the top of the hill to visit the temple, which is said to have some very interesting and unusual artwork. The Chinese faculty members who have gone along as guides and interpreters are especially excited, since this temple is a bit out of the way and is rarely included on tours. Afterward, everyone will take a different path down to meet the bus at the back entrance.

One member of the group, Renata Fields, is in her sixties, and her knees have been giving her trouble for years. She is unable to climb steep hills or more than a dozen or so steps without considerable effort and pain. Also, Renata has lived alone for many years, and she tires of being part of a big group all day long, though she does enjoy these little trips. She notices a map that indicates that, in addition to the path up the hill to the temple and down the other side, there is one other path that goes around the base of the hill. It occurs to Renata that this is a perfect opportunity for her to avoid climbing all those steps and at the same time spend a pleasant hour alone. She tells Mr. Cheng, the man from the Foreign Affairs Office who is in charge of the expedition, about her plan. Mr. Cheng immediately calls to Dai Juan, the youngest English-speaking Chinese guide, and tells her to accompany Renata.

Dai Juan is very disappointed to miss the rare opportunity of seeing this special temple, but she understands Mr. Cheng's request and cheerfully leaves the group to join Renata. Mr. Cheng and Dai Juan are shocked when Renata responds angrily that she does not need or want a companion for her walk, and they are even more surprised when the other Americans seem to sympathize with Renata. Mr. Cheng is at a loss.

Drawing on your knowledge of these two cultures, explain to everyone why there has been a misunderstanding.

1.   Renata can plainly see that Dai Juan does not want to go with her, and she does not want to be accompanied by someone who is going to sulk.

2.   Renata thinks it is wrong for Dai Juan to miss out on the fun just because she is the youngest. Renata thinks that Mr. Cheng

should accompany her himself. After all, she is older than any-one else in the group and should be treated with more respect.

3. Mr. Cheng is afraid that Renata will get lost. Renata, on the other hand, is sure that the path will take her to the meeting place, whether or not she has a Chinese guide along with her.

4. Mr. Cheng, like many Chinese, feels that to leave someone alone is to neglect them. Especially since Renata is older, Mr. Cheng feels that she should be well looked after.

Explanations for Off on Her Own begin on page 79.

7   How Much Work Is Hard Work?

A team of four Chinese scholars from a large and prestigious university were in Honolulu for ten days to meet with six American colleagues from several different U.S. universities. The ten scholars were getting together to finish up a project that they had been working on together for more than three years. The data had been collected, with great effort and many bureaucratic tangles, in several counties in central China. The Chinese team had been tireless and superhumanly patient in working out every problem, so that the data collection had been extremely successful.

Now the researchers had been working separately for nearly a year on analyses, reports, and papers based on their data. The Americans felt very lucky to have obtained the financial and institutional support to give the group the opportunity to get together one last time—this time in the United States—to read each other's papers, work out problems with the analyses, fill in missing bits of information that the other side had, and make sure that everything had been handled in a politically sensitive way. They were to meet for ten days.

The Chinese delegation arrived on Friday morning and were installed in a comfortable, inexpensive hotel in Waikiki. When the Americans arrived late in the afternoon, everyone was eager to talk about what they had been doing and to begin work. They met for dinner and got right down to business at the home of one of the researchers, who had recently taken a job at the University of Hawai'i. Since everyone was tired from traveling, they quit at ten o'clock, but on Saturday morning they were back to work at nine. By one o'clock, the Chinese were getting very distracted. The interpreter, Zhao Wen-Shu, a Chinese who had been in the United States about six years and was married to an American, suggested that everyone break for lunch, but he was ignored. The Americans called out for pizza at two and kept arguing, writing, calculating, and discussing straight through the late lunch. At seven, the Chinese were sent back to their hotel, at their request; the Americans didn't get back to the hotel until ten.

Sunday was, as planned, another workday. The Chinese participated actively in the discussion in the morning and after lunch, which at Zhao Wen-Shu's urging was served at one o'clock. By six, however, the Chinese were anxious to return to the hotel, though the Americans were equally anxious to keep working.

On Monday morning, the Chinese announced that they were taking the afternoon off. The Americans were rather annoyed, since they felt very pressured to get as much as possible accomplished in the short time they had together, but they agreed to arrange a car for the Chinese.

The next two days the Chinese worked hard and cheerfully all day and into the evening, though they insisted on taking off a full hour for lunch right at noon and another for dinner promptly at six, even when they were in the middle of something. The Americans lunched on the doughnuts and fruit provided at the conference center and kept on working. The interpreter could sense tension and resentment building between the two groups. Finally, on Wednesday morning, the Chinese told the interpreter to announce that after Friday at noon they were not going to work any more, that they were going to spend the last forty-eight hours sightseeing. The Americans were clearly annoyed, and they protested. Zhao Wen-Shu decided it was time to step outside his role of interpreter and intervene.

How might Zhao Wen-Shu explain the behavior of each group to the other?

1. The Chinese do not travel often and may suffer much more severely from jet lag than do Americans, who are more accustomed to airplane travel. The Americans should have taken this into account and planned a lighter schedule for the beginning of the week.

2. The Chinese are not accustomed to working as hard as Americans are. No one in China ever works more than seven or eight hours in a day. The Americans should have known this from the time they spent in China.

3. Chinese scholars who travel abroad expect the trip to be a combination of business and pleasure. There is no such thing as a trip that is all business.

4. Many Chinese believe that it is impossible to do good work unless they eat well and regularly and spend a certain amount of time relaxing. To work long hours without eating is considered foolish and counterproductive.

5. The Americans are being very poor hosts by Chinese standards. When the Americans were in China, the Chinese scholars labored intensively to see that the research went smoothly. They expected to be rewarded, not enslaved.

Explanations for How Much Work Is Hard Work? begin on page 81.

8   Welcome Guest Village

Gwen and Brian Gausmann were visiting a small city in eastern China. Since they had wanted to avoid staying in the overpriced "Foreign Guests House," which they had heard via the grapevine was dirty and damp, they were very happy when they found a small hotel that would allow them to stay one night in a clean, inexpensive room overlooking a river. They enjoyed the sunset from the window of their room and congratulated themselves on their cleverness and good fortune.

Just after five o'clock in the morning, while it was still dark, they were awakened by loud knocking on their door and voices. Gwen, who spoke Chinese, answered the door to find a middle-aged woman accompanied by a younger man. The woman told Gwen that she and Brian would have to move to the Foreign Guests House immediately.

When Gwen sleepily asked why, the woman flew into a rage. She shouted at Gwen that there was a car waiting and that they must leave at once, that foreigners were not allowed to stay in this hotel but must stay in the Guests House. "*You guiding! You guiding!*" she kept repeating. "Those are the regulations!"

Gwen calmly refused to leave until the reason for this regulation was explained to her. She wanted to know what possible rationale there could be for insisting that they go at once, when they had already spent the better part of the night there. The woman angrily insisted that the hotel in which they were staying did not meet the high standards of hygiene set by the government for foreign visitors; only the Foreign Guests House did.

Gwen countered that since they had already spent nearly the whole night in the hotel, it could hardly harm them any to finish the night there. She couldn't resist adding that she found the hygiene at this place unexceptionable but that the mold in the rugs at the Foreign Guests House had made a friend of hers sneeze for two days. At this point, the woman became so angry that Gwen thought she would have a stroke, but Gwen was so annoyed that she didn't much care. Finally, Gwen convinced the young man to drag off his raging colleague by insisting that they were completely unprepared to move to another hotel at that hour, but that they would be sure to do so when it was really morning. The old woman, still shouting over her shoulder as she went down the stairs, left Gwen—herself quietly furious and fully awake—and Brian.

What cultural assumptions were behind the woman's anger and her insistence that Gwen and Brian move to the Foreign Guests House?

1. The Chinese rise very early. The woman was incredulous that two able-bodied people were still in bed after five o'clock in the morning; their laziness infuriated her.

2. The woman's position probably made her responsible for Gwen and Brian's health and welfare. She was really worried about the low standards of hygiene in the Chinese hotel, and their refusal to comply with her very reasonable request angered her.

3. Regulations of this type are not negotiable in the minds of the Chinese bureaucrats who must enforce them. The Chinese woman was angered by Gwen's repeated requests for an explanation or a reason for the regulation.

4. Gwen and Brian broke a rule that every foreigner in China knows, and the Chinese woman was justifiably angry. Foreigners are never allowed to stay in Chinese hotels if there is a Foreign Guests House, and they should not have tried. That they would not rectify their error by getting out immediately when they were discovered was truly maddening to the Chinese woman, who was, after all, only enforcing the law.

5. The woman was very angry that Gwen and Brian were cheating their small town out of money she felt they deserved.

Explanations for Welcome Guest Village begin on page 82.

9   Misinterpreted Disappearance

Jesse Waterman, a thirty-year-old expert in special education from a charity foundation in Boston, was a little disappointed when arrangements for her to lecture in Thailand were canceled. Instead she was sent to conduct a series of teacher-training seminars in China's Hebei and Heilongjiang Provinces for two months on an exchange program between her organization and its sister organization in China, the Mingtian Foundation, headquartered in Hangzhou. She had never been to China and knew very little about it. Unfortunately, the sudden change of plans gave her little opportunity to learn more before she left.

At the Shanghai airport Jesse met her Chinese interpreter, Ma Wei-qiang, and some officers from Mingtian, who expressed surprise that Jesse was a young woman. From her name they had expected a man. Jesse spoke no Chinese at all, and the Chinese experts with whom she was working spoke very little English. As a consequence, she spent almost all of her time with Xiao Ma, as everyone called Ma Wei-qiang. She found he was a great cultural informant as well as a competent interpreter and a friendly, helpful guide. Although she was entirely dependent on Xiao Ma for every aspect of her life, from giving the lectures to shopping for a comb to finding a public toilet, she did not feel terribly constrained, since Xiao Ma was always available and always cheerful. On several occasions he worked late into the night with Jesse in her hotel room, translating the final exam papers for the sessions so that Jesse could grade them in time to hand them back at the closing ceremonies. In spite of her early uncertainty, Jesse felt the training sessions were going extremely well, and through Xiao Ma she began to get to know her Chinese-speaking colleagues and develop relationships with them.

After three weeks, she was actually starting to have fun. She began to get braver about exploring in the small cities where they were conducting training sessions, and nearly every night she would cajole Xiao Ma into letting her take him to some inexpensive restaurant so that she could sample the local cuisine. Sometimes one of the other Chinese came along, but usually they went alone so that they could speak English more freely. When the group went on short sight-seeing expeditions, Jesse enjoyed sitting with Xiao Ma in the bus and learning more about China in general and special education in particular. She was also interested in all that he told her about his life as a student and then as an interpreter for Mingtian. Even though communication in English was painstaking, she made sure, on several occasions, to tell the

Chinese expert in charge of the workshops how happy she was with Xiao Ma's interpreting skills and generosity with his time.

Jesse was surprised and upset when, the first morning after the group's arrival in Harbin, she was introduced to her new interpreter, Pan Ming-Ming. When she asked where Ma Wei-qiang had gone, she was simply told that he was needed on another project and had been replaced by Miss Pan. She was shocked that she had not been told that he would be replaced and that he had not even said good-bye. She got along well with Pan Ming-Ming and found her interpreting skills to be almost as good as Xiao Ma's, though Pan Ming-Ming knew considerably less about special education and sometimes had trouble with the technical vocabulary. Still, Jesse was disturbed by Xiao Ma's sudden disappearance. She was even more unsettled, when the group visited the Hangzhou office at the end of the tour, to learn that he had spent the remainder of the summer working in the office on no particular project at all.

Explain to Jesse what happened to Xiao Ma.

1. Because of Jesse's total dependency on Xiao Ma, the authorities at Mingtian Foundation feared that he would be overworked. They were concerned that Xiao Ma would soon be suffering from exhaustion. Jesse should have been more considerate about the number of hours she asked Xiao Ma to work.

2. It is highly unusual for the Chinese to provide a visiting expert with an interpreter of the opposite sex. The Mingtian Foundation had made a mistake and they rectified it at the earliest opportunity.

3. Jesse's behavior toward Xiao Ma was quite intimate by Chinese standards. The Chinese who were with them on the trip were beginning to think that she was interested in him in other than professional ways. Xiao Ma was quietly removed from a situation that might have ruined his reputation.

4. Jesse made a cultural blunder by praising the member with the lowest status on the team to the member with the highest status. The expert in charge of the workshops lost face when she did so. When she continued to praise the interpreter and not the other members of the team, the morale of the rest of the staff suffered, so the leaders thought it wise to replace Xiao Ma.

5. It is common practice in China for personnel to be changed suddenly without explanation. Jesse should not feel that the change of interpreter had anything to do with her.

Explanations for Misinterpreted Disappearance begin on page 84.

Explanations for the Incidents in Part Three

5   Where's the Bus?

1. There is some truth in this explanation, but it is not the best answer. It is highly unlikely that the Foreign Affairs Office could have found out in advance about an emergency regulation, since it was probably put into effect at the last minute, when the Hangzhou authorities realized that more traffic was pouring into the city than was manageable. At the same time, they did try to bluff their way out and expected the foreign teachers to go along with the change of plans, not to question it. Chinese tourists are far less likely to protest a change of plans or ask for a complete explanation than are Westerners. The Chinese view is that if the people in charge make a change, they probably know what they are doing, they probably are taking the best interests of the group into account, and they are most likely doing the best they can so there is no need to ask for an account. They would therefore have accepted almost any explanation for the change, whether they actually believed it or not, allowing their guides to save face if need be.

    It might have been nice if the foreign teachers had gone along with the bluff, but to expect them to do so was unrealistic. Protecting others' face in this way is not part of their cultural conditioning. Furthermore, they were confused and didn't know what, exactly, they were going along with. In many contexts, their experience had told them, such gullible compliance could be rather dangerous.

2. This is one of two good answers. The Foreign Affairs Office was afraid that the foreign teachers would be annoyed by the inconvenience of having to catch the city bus, and they felt embarrassed that they were not able to keep to their original plan. Besides, they didn't want the foreign teachers to know about China's "backwardness." There is an old Chinese saying, "Family scandal should be kept within the family." Their course of action seemed very natural to them, as an effort to maintain face.

    Many Chinese bureaucrats, especially those in jobs like the Foreign Affairs Office, feel personally embarrassed when China is seen by foreign visitors to be backward (Tomlinson

1999). In this case they may have felt ashamed that Hangzhou was not like a modern Western city, able to handle the tremendous flow of traffic generated on a holiday. They hoped that they could withhold this information from their foreign visitors. What they failed to appreciate, since many of them had never traveled outside of China, was that China's backwardness is evident in many ways they had never even considered, and that any foreigner living in China for any length of time becomes quite understanding of such limitations and may even admire the clever solutions to the problems of overpopulation and limited resources that the Chinese come up with on a daily basis. Ironically, their desire to maintain face backfired, causing them to lose face because their foreign charges blamed them, not for the inconvenience, but for being duplicitous.

3.   This is the best answer. The expectation of the Foreign Affairs Office staff, based on experience in their own culture, was that the foreign teachers would understand that an unforeseen problem had arisen when they were given an implausible explanation. The foreign teachers, on the other hand, might have been mildly annoyed to learn the truth, but they would not have blamed the Foreign Affairs Office people and might, indeed, have been completely understanding, since it was out of their hosts' hands to do anything about it. Their cultural conditioning had led them to expect, and prefer, thorough, honest explanations of what had gone wrong (Choi, Nisbett, and Norenzayan 1999). The source of their anger at their Chinese hosts was "not being treated as rational adults." Note that the interpreters, who were foreign language teachers and thus might have been expected to be more sensitive to cultural differences than were the Foreign Affairs Office staff, felt compelled to provide an explanation, even though it got them into trouble with the Foreign Affairs Office staff.

4.   This is not a good answer. The foreign teachers would not have been placated by strangers telling transparent lies. What they wanted was a rational explanation. In fact, the interpreters served (not very successfully in this case, unfortunately) as cultural informants for both the teachers and the

Foreign Affairs Office. Were one or more of them able to do this more effectively by providing (a) a more detailed analysis based on cultural expectations regarding the amount of explanation that was appropriate in this situation (from both points of view) and (b) the possible reasons the Chinese might have had for not wanting to provide a clearer explanation, the holiday might have been a success after all.

5. This is definitely not a good answer. While it is true that what is considered duplicity in one culture may be considered good manners in another, neither the Chinese nor Westerners are likely to consider lying, per se, moral and ethical. The issue here is differences in what constitutes a white lie, or face-saving device, in different cultures. While the Chinese felt they were telling white lies, and it was impolite of the Westerners to acknowledge that they understood that they were being lied to, the Westerners felt that they were being humiliated by being told lies that any child could see through.

6 Off on Her Own

1. Although Dai Juan may have betrayed her disappointment, there is no evidence that she is sulking or being unpleasant; in fact she is cheerful, and she understands the reason for Mr. Cheng's request. Furthermore, the reason for her being on the trip is to act as a guide and interpreter. It is not specifically Dai Juan's company that Renata is objecting to but any company. She wishes to be alone. This desire to be alone is one that neither Dai Juan nor Mr. Cheng is likely to anticipate or understand. Please choose again.

2. This is quite possibly Mr. Cheng's interpretation of the incident, but it is not likely that Renata has this in mind. Mr. Cheng's cultural upbringing has led him to believe that older people will assume their right to special, more respectful treatment. Respect for elders is one of the most important teachings of Confucius, a teaching that survived the Communist Revolution pretty much intact (Fang 1999). Renata, on the other hand, expects to be treated as the physical and mental equal of anyone else in the group (i.e., the younger teachers) until she presents incontrovertible evidence to the con-

trary. She wants only to be alone, but this is not a possibility that Mr. Cheng has been culturally conditioned to consider.

3. This is a possible answer but not the most likely. Mr. Cheng is responsible for all of the foreign visitors in his care, and this is a heavy responsibility. If something untoward happens to Renata, Mr. Cheng will be in big trouble with his superiors. If she gets lost and everyone has to look for her, thus delaying the departure of the bus and interfering with the enjoyment of the other tourists, he will be blamed for the unsuccessful trip. Therefore, even though it is unlikely that she will stray from the only available path, Mr. Cheng does not like to take chances. In Renata's culture, adults are responsible for their own behavior and it is insulting to suggest, even indirectly, that she might get lost or even hold up the departure of the bus. Renata assumes that as an adult, she is responsible for herself, whereas Mr. Cheng assumes that he is responsible for her. Still, since there is only one path that leads around the base of the mountain to where the bus is waiting, and no side paths, there is a better alternative.

4. This is the best answer. According to his cultural conditioning, Mr. Cheng is behaving appropriately. Renata is an older guest and should therefore be given special consideration. Chinese, like all collectivists, do not as a rule enjoy being alone (Gao and Ting-Toomey 1998); at the very least it would be considered slightly odd to wish to be alone when there was someone to accompany you. In addition, because of Renata's age and her bad knees, both Mr. Cheng and Dai Juan assume—quite naturally in their culture—that Renata will appreciate an arm to lean on as she walks. Renata interprets his concern as a lack of trust; maybe Mr. Cheng thinks she is too old and infirm to take care of herself. In Renata's culture, the only reason that tour guides would be unwilling to let a guest out of their sight would be because they thought she would do something illegal or foolish. Also, in Renata's culture, it is generally inappropriate to make a point of a person's advanced age or to imply that he or she may be in need of assistance.

7 How Much Work Is Hard Work?

1. While it is true that the average Chinese person does not
    travel as far or as often as an American, it cannot be assumed
    that these particular Chinese scholars are not well traveled,
    nor can it be assumed that Chinese people suffer more from
    jet lag than Americans do. Look for an alternative that takes
    cultural differences into account.

2. This is not a good alternative. These particular Americans
    had been able to observe their Chinese colleagues' hard work
    to make the data collection a success. In general, the Chi-
    nese are certainly no strangers to hard work and often work
    from early in the morning to late at night. Look for a better
    alternative.

3. This is the best of several good answers. A trip abroad is a
    great treat for many Chinese, including respected academ-
    ics, who may have few opportunities and limited personal
    resources for international travel. There is considerable pres-
    tige involved in foreign travel. Therefore, being able to dem-
    onstrate, upon their return, that they were treated well may
    be a matter of some importance. It would involve a loss of
    face (Earley 1997) to admit that all they did was work dur-
    ing their stay in Hawai'i; they must be able to say that they
    visited some of the famous tourist attractions that other col-
    leagues may have seen on similar junkets. This does not mean
    that the Chinese scholars did not come prepared to work,
    and work hard, as can be seen in the details of the incident.

    Although this incident focuses on a particular situation,
    it is common for Chinese to comment on the "craziness" of
    the American pace of life, which often does not allow time
    to chat with friends, enjoy nutritious meals, or have a good
    night's sleep when one is tired.

4. This is one of several good answers. Chinese people don't
    share the American view that going without sleep, skipping
    meals, or eating whatever junk food is on hand is a virtue,
    indicating dedication and a good work ethic. Even very hard-
    working Chinese take time out to have a good breakfast, a
    substantial lunch, and a light but nutritious supper. Some
    very productive people still take time out for a *xiuxi*, or si-

esta, after lunch. In fact, a two-hour lunch break, long enough to allow all workers to xiuxi, or at least relax, is built into the Chinese workday. While the Chinese may work very long hours for a short period of time to accomplish some particular task, for sustained efforts moderation is considered a much more efficient approach (Chinese Culture Connection 1987). In general, the Chinese will strive to achieve a sense of balance in their activities.

5. This is one of several good answers. The Americans seem to assume that, because the Chinese behaved one way as hosts, they will behave the same way as guests. The Americans are ignoring something of which they should, as sinologists and speakers of the Chinese language, be aware. International travel is not merely a means to achieve some particular end— give a paper at a conference, view a plant in operation, or drive a bargain—but a source of considerable prestige in and of itself. As part of their thinking about traveling overseas for business, Chinese people anticipate opportunities for sightseeing and enjoying local entertainment.

8   Welcome Guest Village

1. This is not a good choice. While it's true that many Chinese rise very early, even when on vacation, just as some Americans are early risers, this would not make the woman angry, at least not furiously so.

2. This is not entirely implausible, but anyone who has seen the accommodations set aside for foreign visitors in small towns will question the strength of this alternative. Theoretically, amenities like hot water and clean linens are to be provided in such places, but the reality is more often moldy carpets (the result of burst water pipes), dirty or missing linens, and no mosquito net where one is desperately needed, simply because someone has somehow learned that "foreigners don't use mosquito nets in their countries." At any rate, her request cannot be considered reasonable in this light because, as Gwen points out, she and Brian had already spent most of the night and whatever damage to their health was going to be done had probably already been done.

Still, the Chinese woman may have been trying to save face, if she was indeed responsible for having failed to notice their presence in town sooner and check on where they were staying. She may still have been able to salvage some face by rousing them at five o'clock in the morning to move them to a "superior" hotel, showing that she was doing her best at her job.

3. This is a good answer. "*You guiding*" is a final answer. To Chinese people it signals that "the authorities," whoever they may be, have made a regulation, and there is no getting around it. Two of the authors use the justification "*You guiding*" to communicate to their children that rules are rules and there will be no discussion. For example, "Why can't I eat my sandwich in the bus?" is answered by "*You guiding*," and pointing to the sign. The children understand that you just don't argue with "*guiding*."

    Gwen enraged the Chinese woman by repeatedly asking her for an explanation of an existing regulation. Chinese officials, especially those charged with carrying out a superior's orders, can get really furious about being asked a simple "why." Gwen's culture has conditioned her to ask for reasons before she takes actions which seem illogical to her. Being asked to move to another hotel at five o'clock in the morning was incomprehensible and, furthermore, she was half asleep, so she was highly unlikely to simply obey, which was what the Chinese woman expected. In the minds of most Chinese, rules and regulations should be followed, not challenged (Chinese Culture Connection). Under a closed, nontransparent political system, laws and regulations are usually developed by a small group of people. Most Chinese consider rules and regulations in the same light as orders from authoritative individuals. To raise questions about existing rules and regulations is equivalent to challenging the authorities, something Gwen did as a matter of course, but which is highly unusual in China. When Gwen kept questioning the Chinese woman about the foreign guest regulation, the woman felt that her authority had been threatened and violated, and she took it very personally.

4. There is some truth in this, though it is not the best answer. Foreigners are generally required to stay in the hotels set aside for their use, especially in smaller towns, but different municipalities enforce the regulations to varying degrees. The fact that Gwen and Brian were allowed to stay in the Chinese hotel in the first place was an indication that the proprietors of that hotel were not expecting any trouble. While the existence of such regulations might be common knowledge, it is also common practice to try to evade them, since the officially approved accommodations are frequently both unhygienic and overpriced and the service contemptuous. Look for an alternative that takes culture into account.

5. Not a good answer, though there may be a grain of truth in it. Many Chinese assume, with some reason, that all foreign visitors are fabulously rich. They cannot comprehend why foreign visitors would begrudge them the profits they make on overcharging them for their accommodations. The Chinese woman may indeed have been annoyed that Gwen and Brian were too cheap to stay in the Foreign Guests House and didn't appreciate the "luxuries" available to them. It would not occur to her that Gwen and Brian might have appreciated a view of the river more than a malfunctioning air conditioner. There is, however, an alternative that is more plausible and reflects the effects of culture.

9   Misinterpreted Disappearance

1. While it might have been nice of Jesse to consider how difficult Xiao Ma's burden as an interpreter was, this is not a likely answer. Interpreters in China are often expected to be something like guardian angels to the foreign visitors they are working with. They are responsible not only for making sure communication is smooth but also for seeing that the visitors' needs are met, that they are having a reasonably enjoyable time, and that the best possible working conditions are provided. They are expected to work around the clock, if that is what the foreign expert requires of them. It is very unlikely that the Mingtian Foundation would consider Xiao Ma's burden too great in this case.

2. You are on the right track. While every effort is made to
    ensure that the Chinese who will be traveling or spending a
    great deal of time with foreign experts (interpreters, contact
    teachers at universities, team-teachers, etc.) are of the same
    sex, there are many occasions where it is not possible or prac-
    tical. It is actually quite common for visiting experts to be
    given interpreters of the opposite sex, but rarely if they are
    both young and single. In this case, Ma Wei-qiang is obvi-
    ously the first choice for the job in terms of specialized knowl-
    edge. Nevertheless, it is true that the Mingtian Foundation
    made a mistake, and that had they known Jesse was a woman,
    they might well have sent Pan Ming-Ming in the first place.
    If other problems had not arisen, however, they would prob-
    ably not have gone to the trouble and expense of changing
    interpreters in the middle of the trip. There is a better an-
    swer.

3. This is the best answer. Jesse behaved in an inappropriately
    intimate manner with Xiao Ma by Chinese standards, caus-
    ing her Chinese colleagues to think she was interested in
    Xiao Ma personally. Xiao Ma was quietly removed from his
    position so that nothing else embarrassing could happen.
    Although political and social changes over the past few de-
    cades have resulted in increasing flexibility, the relationship
    between male and female colleagues is still a very sensitive
    issue (see A Night at the Opera, pages 102–103 for a discus-
    sion of this point). It becomes even more sensitive when a
    foreigner is involved. Xiao Ma's boss felt he had a responsi-
    bility to protect Xiao Ma from ruining his reputation by get-
    ting involved with an American woman.

    There are a number of ways in which Jesse's behavior
    led her Chinese colleagues to misinterpret her relationship
    with Ma Wei-qiang. Inviting her interpreter to dinner once
    or twice would seem to the Chinese to be a nice expression
    of gratitude, but inviting him daily and rarely including any
    of the others would seem to the Chinese to indicate a desire
    for privacy, and thus personal interest. In Jesse's mind, she
    was not compromising Xiao Ma because (a) dinnertime was
    time off, and she could spend it as she liked; naturally she
    wanted to spend it either alone or with the one person she

could really talk to; (b) she was not spending very much money by her standards, but unless she had treated Xiao Ma, he couldn't have afforded to join her so often; and (c) all the places they went to were public. Even if it were less relaxing, Jesse should have included others in the group going to dinner. Dining alone with someone is considered quite intimate by Chinese standards, and doing so in a public place is tantamount to declaring that the relationship itself is public, in other words, a serious and permanent one.

Jesse also misunderstood the purpose of the group outings, which were arranged to give the team a chance to bond and have fun together (Bhawuk 1998). Even though it might have been tiring, she should have sat with the non-English-speaking members of the group and attempted to converse, however lamely. She saw the outings, again, as "time off" and relaxed in Xiao Ma's company. She also saw this time off as a chance to learn other things about China, things she felt she couldn't learn from her non-English-speaking colleagues. To the Chinese, however, she appeared to have eyes only for Xiao Ma.

While it is understandable, given the time constraints, that Jesse and Xiao Ma would need to work late into the night together, Jesse would have been wise to invite others to drop by to have a look at the exams or "consult" with them, if only to assure the others that their late hours together were all work and no play. Having the others stop by might actually have added to Jesse and Xiao Ma's workload, since it would have aggravated the time pressure on them, but it would have been worth the investment in everyone's peace of mind. At the very least, a conspicuously open door would have alleviated suspicions.

It should be noted that it is very possible that Xiao Ma himself asked to be removed from the scene. Word gets around, and we have known interpreters who returned to furious spouses, boyfriends, or girlfriends, all because of what others wrote home to friends during a trip about the "warm relationship" between the foreign expert and the interpreter. By discussing the situation with his superiors, Xiao Ma would have been saying that he was *not* carrying on with this foreign expert and was concerned about his reputation, all of which would reflect well upon him in his job. He would also be more likely to be trusted in the future if he refused to be placed in this increasingly compromising position (Fukuyama 1995).

4. This is not a good choice. There was no cultural reason for Jesse not to praise Xiao Ma to his superiors. Praise for individual members of a team is not out of line, unless it is meant as an indirect method of pointing to the shortcomings of another team member. There is no evidence that this was what Jesse was doing. In fact, she was working smoothly with her Chinese colleagues and, with Xiao Ma's assistance, getting to know them. Indeed, given the difficult and demanding job that Xiao Ma had been doing, it would have been rather impolite for her not to mention her satisfaction with his efforts. Her praise of Xiao Ma did create a problem, but only in combination with a number of other behaviors.

5. This answer is partially correct. Western visitors to China often find that personnel appear and disappear for no apparent reason, and no explanation is ever given. In the situation described above, however, such a change would have been unlikely. This was a small group, working closely together and traveling from place to place. A change of personnel would have been difficult and expensive to organize. Also, Xiao Ma was clearly the better choice as an interpreter for this particular group. The sudden change of interpreter *did* have something to do with Jesse.

One of our Chinese authors has suggested that perhaps we could say that sudden changes of personnel with little or no notice are normal in the Chinese workplace, but that such changes usually indicate impending scandal. When people are quietly transferred or suddenly disappear from organizations, very possibly their superiors are trying to cover up things for them. There is a Chinese saying, "*Jiachou buke waiyang*," which means "Family scandals must be kept within." The Chinese believe that anything that can potentially cause embarrassment should be dealt with quietly and within the confines of the collective. In this case insiders would have known, or at least suspected, the reasons for Xiao Ma's disappearance, but would never have discussed them with outsiders.

Part Four

The Workplace:
Understanding Relationships
with Colleagues

10   The Dinner Invitation

After a couple of months in China, Jason seemed to be settling down somewhat. He was still excited and pleased with his company's decision to transfer him to the main office in Shanghai. The city was very crowded, but there were some interesting places to visit, and he was enjoying the opportunity to practice his Chinese. Although he had studied Chinese for two years while enrolled at the university, it almost seemed like a new language upon his arrival in China. Still, he was making good progress.

One person he was thankful for was Cao Jianfa. Xiao Cao, as everyone called him, worked with Jason in finance, and had really helped him get acquainted with the office and, to some extent, with Shanghai. Xiao Cao's English was much better than Jason's Chinese, which allowed them to communicate fairly well in English. Xiao Cao had picked Jason up at the airport upon his arrival and showed him how to commute to work, accompanying Jason during the first week. Xiao Cao had invited Jason to lunch on several occasions, showing him the good places to eat, and had also invited him to dinner or other evening social activities a few times. Their conversations had ranged from matters at the office to their families. They also coached each other in their language development. At the office they worked well together, sharing responsibility for several finance projects and analyses.

Jason thought it would be a good idea to invite Xiao Cao to dinner at a nice restaurant for helping him out so much, so he asked Xiao Cao if he would like to go to dinner on Friday. Xiao Cao responded in Chinese, "*Dui bu qi, you shi,*" meaning literally, "I'm sorry, I have things (to do)." Jason, feeling the answer was a little cold, was curious about what Xiao Cao had to do that would prevent him from going out to dinner, so he asked, "Are you busy? Working late?" Xiao Cao, seeming a little uneasy, responded, "No, I just have some things to take care of." Jason, sensing the uneasiness in the conversation, became puzzled and a little frustrated. Not wanting to create a bad situation, he said to Xiao Cao, "Well, when you'd like to, maybe we can go out some-time...."

During the remainder of the week, Jason felt a bit awkward around Xiao Cao. He spent the weekend by himself and could not keep from wondering why Xiao Cao did not seem interested in going to dinner with him. What might explain Xiao Cao's behavior?

1. In China, it is only appropriate for the host colleague to invite the foreign colleague to evening social events.

2. Xiao Cao was simply carrying out his initial responsibility to introduce Jason to a few places, but he had no further interest in a personal relationship with Jason.

3. Xiao Cao had to work Friday evening but was embarrassed to divulge this to Jason because, to the Chinese, working late means that one is not working productively during the day.

4. Xiao Cao felt that he had developed a trusting relationship with Jason and, as such, could trust Jason to understand when he had "things."

5. By saying that he had "things," Xiao Cao was implying that he had to take care of some personal affairs. Xiao Cao did not wish to specify them because by doing so, he would reveal the relative importance of various personal affairs compared with Jason's request.

Explanations for The Dinner Invitation begin on page 100.

11 A Night at the Opera

"It's taken a long time, but I think I'm ready," Bill Rourke said to himself as he got off the plane in Taipei. Bill had indeed worked hard over a number of years preparing himself for a successful business career that would hopefully incorporate a number of overseas assignments. He was in Taipei to work for a firm that would produce fashionable women's wear for the American and Canadian markets, with possible additions of select European markets in the future. Bill had studied Chinese in college, had earned an MBA at a school that specialized in international business, and had worked for two years in the fashion industry in New York City. He was ready to make his mark with this opportunity in Taipei. Given his professional ambitions, he had put off marriage and starting a family, even though he had enjoyed an active social life in college, graduate school, and his two years in New York.

Bill found his coworkers to be quite friendly and appreciative of his considerable conversational skill in Chinese. Workers frequently socialized with each other, for instance, going out to dinner together in groups of ten or twelve. Bill was often asked to join these groups. After about two months Bill and a female coworker named Li Song found themselves exchanging smiles at these social gatherings. Bill and Li Song worked in different departments, so they did not necessarily see each other every workday. However, Bill felt that Li Song showed an interest in a one-on-one interaction, or what he would call a "date," through her smiles at these group gatherings. One day at work, Bill went to Li Song's department, found that she wasn't too busy at the moment, and asked her to go with him to the opera. Li Song agreed.

In the days following the evening at the opera, Bill sensed that other people had changed their behaviors slightly when interacting with him. For example, other women who used to be friendly became slightly more formal and businesslike in their interactions with him.

If Bill asked you for cultural information that might help him interpret what was happening, what would you say?

1. Bill must have behaved badly toward Li Song at the opera. She told her friends about his behavior. That's why all of the others are treating Bill strangely.

2. Li Song, and others who knew of the evening at the opera, interpreted this social interaction as a very serious move toward a romantic relationship.

3. Both Li Song and Bill should have requested the approval of their immediate supervisors before engaging in a social interaction such as an evening at the opera.

4. An evening at the opera has a special meaning in Chinese culture compared with an evening at a movie or a restaurant.

Explanations for A Night at the Opera begin on page 102.

12   Two Invitations

To take advantage of lower labor costs, Tom Chung's company in San Francisco sent him to work with one of its major suppliers in Shanghai. The company, Souvenirs Forever, manufactured and imported small gift items that tourists bought as mementos of their trips. The company executives sent Tom because they thought a Chinese American would be able to develop close business relationships quickly.

Tom became friendly with a coworker, Wang Jun, who was at about his level in the company. Wang Jun enjoyed Tom's company because of a common interest in chess and because they had fun exchanging informal language lessons. Wang Jun and Tom had agreed to play a game of chess, speaking half the time in Chinese and half the time in English, on a certain Tuesday evening. In anticipation Tom had bought a new chess set made of carved marble. On that Tuesday afternoon, however, Wang Jun told Tom that he couldn't play chess that evening because his superior at work had asked him to go to dinner with him. He gave no other explanation.

Tom was irritated and thought to himself, I'm being blown off. However, he knew enough about differences between China and the United States to ask, "I wonder if there is something cultural involved here." If Tom asked you for help in interpreting this incident, what would you say?

1. There is a cultural difference, and it focuses on the importance of invitations to dinner.

2. There is a cultural difference, and it focuses on the role of Chinese Americans living in China.

3. There is a cultural difference, and it focuses on Chinese who choose to spend their free time learning English.

4. There is a cultural difference, and it focuses on the importance of hierarchies.

Explanations for Two Invitations begin on page 103.

13   Share the Wealth

Joe Kingsley had been working for a Chinese-owned and -operated company in Bengbu for about six months. The division he was working in had a small collection of Chinese-English dictionaries, English-language reference books and novels, and some videos in English, including a couple of training films and several feature films that Joe had brought at his new employer's request when he came from Iowa. Joe knew that some of the other divisions in the company had similar collections. He had sometimes used his friendship with one of the guys in another department, Gu Bing, to borrow English novels and reference books, and in return he had let Gu Bing borrow books from his section's collection. On other occasions, he had seen friendly, noisy exchanges, where one of the other workers in his division had lent a book or video to a colleague from another section.

Joe thought it was a great idea when a memo was circulated saying that the company's leaders had decided to collect all the English-language materials together into a single collection and put them in a small room that was currently being used for storage, so that all employees could have equal access to them. Now he would no longer have to go from department to department trying to find the materials he needed.

Joe was very surprised to hear his co-workers complaining about the new policy and was astounded to see them hiding most of the books and all but one of the videos in their desks when the young man in charge came to the department to collect their English-language materials. When Joe checked out the new so-called collection, he found that the few items there were all outdated or somehow damaged. He also noticed that none of the materials he had borrowed from Gu Bing were in the collection. He asked his friend why the Chinese were unwilling to share their English-language materials with all of their co-workers, when they had seemed willing to share them within their departments and with individuals from other departments.

What explanation do you think Gu Bing gave Joe?

1.   By restricting access to their materials, co-workers in each section were able to maintain a certain necessary control over their colleagues.

2.   This was not normal behavior among Chinese co-workers. Something was very wrong with the relationships among the people in the different departments. Joe hadn't noticed this

because he was an outsider and couldn't detect the subtle signals.

3.   The workers simply felt it would be inconvenient for them if they had to go to another room every time they needed English-language materials.

4.   The workers in each division felt that they needed to keep their materials so that they had something valuable to exchange when they needed information or help from colleagues in another section.

5.   Joe didn't understand that the divisions in Chinese companies are in much greater competition with one another than are similar divisions in an American company.

Explanations for Share the Wealth begin on page 105.

14　Got a Match?

Georgia London was enjoying her job at a Chinese American joint-venture company. She was surprised by how modern and up-to-date her colleagues were. Some of the Chinese she worked with, who were in their twenties and early thirties, seemed more cosmopolitan than her friends back at home in Houston.

One Monday her office mate, Lü Xiaohong, told Georgia that she was going to be getting married in about two months and that she hoped Georgia would come to her wedding. Georgia was very surprised, as she had had no idea that Xiaohong even had a boyfriend. Xiaohong explained that up until three weeks ago she *hadn't* had a boyfriend. Her parents had consulted with an old woman in the neighborhood, who sometimes worked as a matchmaker, to find a suitable boy for Xiaohong to marry. Xiaohong and her parents had been introduced to the young man the matchmaker had chosen and his parents three Sundays earlier, and in the last three weeks the two young people had met five times to go out for a walk and talk together. They had decided that the match would work and had announced their decision to get married.

Georgia was stunned. To her knowledge, she had never met anyone who had an arranged marriage, and while she knew that some Chinese still used matchmakers to arrange their marriages, she had assumed it was a phenomenon restricted to backward countryside areas. Xiaohong told her that arranged marriages weren't very common in the city, but neither would most people think that the 10 to 20 percent of couples who get together that way are odd.

How might Lü Xiaohong explain to Georgia her reasons for relying on her parents and a matchmaker to find a husband?

1. Young people are likely to make big mistakes in such important matters as choosing a spouse or a career. They should listen to their elders in such matters.

2. Many urban Chinese are still pretty backward. They follow old traditions without thinking too much about them.

3. The traditional ways really are better. A girl should be obedient to her father and brothers until she marries and then be obedient to her husband. This is not inconsistent with having a full-time career and a cosmopolitan view of life.

4. No one knows you better or has your interests more at heart than your parents. With the benefit of their experience, they are likely to choose a better spouse for you than you could choose for yourself.

Note: Several of the Chinese to whom we showed the incidents early on complained that this incident was "stupid" and that such situations are very rare. They seemed really bothered by the incident and were uncomfortable with its inclusion in the materials. We considered dropping it, but the very fact that it aroused so much emotion intrigued us. In addition, all of the authors had encountered arranged marriages, so we included the incident in the validation sample. The incident validated well, supporting our interpretations.

Explanations for Got a Match? begin on page 106.

15   Is More Expected of Leaders?

Greg Rossi, originally from Boston, Massachusetts, was in Nanjing working with executives from a fine dinnerware manufacturer on a plan to develop new designs that should be popular in the North American market. Although he worked with a number of executives, his chief counterpart was Zhang Zhi-hao, whose subordinates referred to him as Lao Zhang. Greg worked well with Lao Zhang for about six months, but then he began to notice that the working relationship was not as effective as it had been. Lao Zhang did not seem to be able to follow through on his commitments to Greg, and it appeared to Greg that Lao Zhang had become unable to provide leadership to his subordinates. This puzzled Greg, because in the earlier stages of their working relationship, Lao Zhang had seemed so respected by his subordinates and by executives at about Lao Zhang's level in the organization. The only possibility that occurred to Greg was that Lao Zhang was spending free time with one of the organization's attractive younger secretaries. It could have been a sexual relationship, but Greg didn't know for sure. This secretary also received a lot of positive attention from Lao Zhang during the workday, but this in itself did not surprise Greg, since she was a very capable worker and, at least in Greg's mind, deserved positive attention for her work. In addition, Greg thought to himself, I met *my* wife at my organization back in Boston, and she was a secretary at the time. We certainly didn't break any rules, and besides, what we did was nobody's business as long as it didn't affect our work. Of course I *was* separated from my first wife at the time, and Lao Zhang isn't.

Are there cultural differences involved in Lao Zhang's current relations with coworkers and in Greg's reactions to Lao Zhang's behavior?

1.   Greg's cultural background, more than Lao Zhang's, guides people into considering the personal morality of leaders when reacting to their directives.

2.   Lao Zhang's cultural background, more than Greg's, guides people into considering the personal morality of leaders when reacting to their directives.

3.   Greg's cultural background, more than Lao Zhang's, guides people into making distinctions between a person's "own business" and what is reasonably the concern of others.

4. Lao Zhang's cultural background, more than Greg's, guides people into making distinctions between a person's "own business" and what is reasonably the concern of others.

5. In China, one's organization is not an appropriate place to meet members of the opposite sex for relationships that may become romantic in nature.

Explanations for Is More Expected of Leaders? begin on page 108.

Explanations for the Incidents in Part Four

10   The Dinner Invitation

1. This statement is simply not true. Social life in China is reciprocal. While it may be easier, initially, for the host colleague to invite the guest colleague simply because the host knows more about the local scene, it is perfectly appropriate (and actually expected) for the guest to reciprocate with something like a dinner invitation, when he or she feels ready to do so.

2. This is not a good answer. While Xiao Cao may have been obligated to show Jason around initially, one cannot conclude from the above incident that Xiao Cao had no further interest in developing a personal relationship with Jason. On the contrary, there is considerable evidence that Xiao Cao did value Jason's companionship and felt quite comfortable with him.

3. This is not a good choice. It is not true that the Chinese consider working late to be evidence of low productivity. To the contrary, the Chinese are generally encouraged to go the extra mile for their organization. Working late is equated with working hard.

4. This is a possible answer. Xiao Cao felt enough trust had been developed between Jason and himself that Jason should have been able to understand when he had "things (to do)." In China, it is very common for people to give ambiguous explanations such as "I have things." The person giving this answer may or may not have specific things to do. However, it is considered to be a polite way of turning down an invitation. People don't expect further questioning when such a reason is given. Chinese people will feel their trustworthiness is challenged if their friends or colleagues try to find out what "things" they have planned.

   Chinese people spend a lot of time, resources, and energy developing a trusting relationship (Fukuyama 1995). Once such a relationship is established, a lot of assumptions will be made. For example, if a Chinese person makes plans to meet her friends for dinner on Sunday night and later finds out for some reason that she cannot attend the dinner, she will tell her friends that she "has things." She will assume her friends will understand that she is missing the dinner for sufficient reasons. She won't need to worry about explaining to them what she will be doing instead of going to dinner with them.

An American will often refuse an invitation from an acquaintance with the phrase "I have other plans." However, in such a case, the relationship is not such a close one as that which has developed between Cao Jianfa and Jason. Jason felt that he and Xiao Cao were buddies and that they were close enough that Xiao Cao should offer a plausible reason when declining an invitation: "Oh, I would love to, but my child is ill and I will be needed at home" or "I'm sorry, but I previously arranged an appointment with some old friends at that time." Even if Xiao Cao had said, "I've got some stuff to do for my dad," Jason would have felt better. Xiao Cao's "I have things" seemed cold to Jason. From Xiao Cao's point of view, however, it is the very closeness of the relationship that allowed him to say no more than "I have things." While Xiao Cao was most likely made uncomfortable by what seemed to him like a lack of trust on Jason's part, Jason probably thought Xiao Cao was being unnecessarily secretive.

Xiao Cao was also protecting his emotional privacy by being unclear about the exact nature of the things he had planned. Chinese people have virtually no personal privacy; they are hardly ever alone. The privacy of their thoughts and plans can be very important to them, and they do not expect to have that emotional privacy challenged by a friend.

5. This is a good answer. By saying that he had "things," Xiao Cao avoided comparing the relative importance between the "things" and Jason's dinner invitation. Such an indirect approach is often adopted by the Chinese to avoid hurting other people's feelings, as a more direct response might do.

There are many other instances in these incidents of the Chinese preference for indirectness and saving face. By simply saying that one has "things," the person declining the invitation is avoiding a situation wherein a comparison might be made as to the relative importance the declining person assigns to the activities in question. Rather than creating a possibly embarrassing situation (and loss of face), it is much more harmonious to give the indirect "I have things."

11   A Night at the Opera

1.   There is absolutely no evidence in the incident to support this explanation. There is a more obvious explanation. Please choose again.

2.   This is a good answer. Bill's Chinese colleagues interpreted his date with Li Song as the beginning of a serious romantic relationship. Confucius taught that men and women without any relationship should not have one-on-one interactions. Now, people interpret this teaching much more flexibly. Especially in the workplace, male-female interactions are considered normal and necessary (Hui and Luk 1997). However, a one-on-one date after work between a man and a woman still carries the specific message that they are romantically involved. Male and female relationships in China are not as open as in most Western societies. Once a man is believed to be involved in a relationship, women usually treat him more formally. The same thing is true for women.

There is less one-on-one "dating around" in most Asian countries compared with North America. In Asia people socialize in groups, as described in the second paragraph of the incident. A Chinese man and a Chinese woman often show special interest in each other through smiles and glances and other forms of nonverbal behavior. But when they decide to separate themselves from the large group and go out on a date alone, they realize that this is a serious step toward a romantic relationship that will be recognized as such by others whom they know. Li Song, then, was likely to take the evening at the opera as a sign that Bill had serious and permanent romantic intentions. Bill, given his experiences in his own culture, was not likely to interpret the evening so seriously and is more likely to call it "just a first date."

This incident, in various forms, takes place frequently among North Americans and Europeans who are simply trying to have adequate social lives during their assignments in Asia. It is the sort of personal, important, and potentially stressful incident that should be explained to people but often is not, given their single-minded task orientation (e.g., business negotiations). In everyday, informal language North Americans and Europeans need to know that a first date is a much bigger deal in China than it is in many other countries.

3. Even though it is true that Chinese supervisors usually play a role in their subordinates' private lives, Bill and Li Song didn't need to ask permission from their supervisors to attend the opera.

   There may be individual supervisors who would prefer to be informed about dates such as this one, but this preference is not so widespread as to be considered part of the culture. Rather, it is a preference that some supervisors have and some do not. There are many examples in Taipei of men and women meeting at work, interacting in large groups, beginning one-on-one dating, and later marrying, all without the involvement of supervisors. Many supervisors do become involved in arranging interactions between eligible men and women, but their participation in the "pairing off" is not essential. Please choose again.

4. There is no special meaning to an evening at the opera. People's reactions to the one-on-one interaction between Li Song and Bill would have occurred if they had gone to a movie, a restaurant, a nightclub, or a sporting event. Please choose again.

12 Two Invitations

1. While dining with others is a common and important activity in China, it has no special meaning in this incident. Wang Jun would have told Tom that he couldn't play chess even if his superior had invited him to some other evening activity, such as a sporting event, theatrical presentation, or lecture at a nearby university. Please choose again.

2. This is not a good answer. Tom's ethnic background is irrelevant, with the possible exception that Wang Jun may have thought that someone who "looks Chinese" would know how to interpret the event. Please choose again.

3. There is no special meaning surrounding the fact that Wang Jun wanted to learn English. All but the most fervently nationalistic Chinese business executives would be pleased that Wang Jun was learning English on his own time. Please choose again.

4. This is a good answer. The importance of knowing, and taking seriously, one's place in society's hierarchy must be understood by Americans who spend time in China (Hsu 1981; Bond 1986). The generalization that should be kept in mind is that the Chinese value hierarchies and strive for clarity in vertical relationships. Americans recognize that some people are bosses and others are subordinates, but they are more comfortable when there is movement toward a horizontal relationship. This generalization has many specific implications. For instance, in the United States many subordinates want to get on a first-name basis with their bosses. In China this is very rare. In the United States many subordinates feel that their free time (after work hours) is their own, and they are not as likely to feel the need to honor requests from superiors that free time be spent in certain ways. In China there is not this sharp distinction between superiors' requests for how time is spent on and off the job, given the emphasis on vertical relationships and the corresponding respect subordinates have for superiors' wishes.

   In this incident Wang Jun received a request from his superior and felt the obligation to honor it. He realized that other Chinese would act in a similar manner, since "My superior asked me to a social event" is a satisfactory explanation when breaking a previous social obligation. Tom, on the other hand, was not socialized in his culture to believe that this was a good excuse and would have told his boss something like "I already have a social engagement. Can we schedule something another time?"

   A related issue is that, in China, superiors are expected to do what is best for their subordinates. If they don't, they are not good superiors. Given this belief, subordinates don't expect that superiors will explain the reasons for their requests. Wang Jun, then, felt that his superior must have had a good reason for inviting him to the social event and that this reason should be respected, even though he might not have known the exact reason when telling Tom that he had to break the engagement. In the United States, if Tom received a last-minute invitation from his boss, before accepting it, he would want to know the exact and highly important reason, so that this information could be passed on to the person with whom he had the previous engagement.

13   Share the Wealth

1. Although Gu Bing would be unlikely to give the situation such a negative interpretation, this is a good answer. The question was not so much one of having control over others as of ensuring cooperation among all by maintaining a balance of power. When access to knowledge or information is restricted, the person who can grant access has a certain power. Everyone in the company understood that if they wanted to get things done, they had to stay on the good side of the people who controlled access to the information (or goods, services, people). They also knew that such relationships were facilitated by the fact that many different people, or departments, had control over valuable materials. Having and keeping power over small things, like having access to a Chinese-English dictionary, contributes to getting and keeping small amounts of power over large numbers of people. This system is reciprocal and is referred to, generally, as *guanxi*. Look for an answer that takes the cooperation angle into account.

2. There is no support for this answer in the incident. Both the friendly exchange of favors between departments and the hoarding of materials within departments are quite normal among Chinese colleagues. Look for a better explanation.

3. While this explanation appears to be reasonable on the surface, remember that Joe felt that it would be *more* convenient for him if the English-language books and videos were all in one location. As it stood prior to the memo, the materials were spread all over the company and had to be sought out one by one. As one of our validators pointed out, however, this is the explanation that Gu Bing would most likely have given to Joe, the real answer being a bit embarrassing,

as Gu Bing may have felt it reflected negatively on the Chinese. Choose another answer.

4. This is the best answer. Chinese relationships are based on a complex system of guanxi, or connections (Luo and Chen 1996; Fang 1999). One way of establishing good guanxi is to exchange favors, small and large, over a long period of time. Often the result of this is that Chinese will withhold information, goods, and services from others, even those with whom they are ostensibly cooperating, such as colleagues or fellow researchers working in the same field at other institutions. If they don't withhold information and access to materials (or even people), then those resources won't be available as bargaining tools later on. It is common practice for a Chinese person who has done someone a favor to make a very specific suggestion as to something that he or she might be offered in exchange in the future to even out the guanxi debt. The Chinese in each division may have feared that by pooling the relatively rare and valuable English-language materials, they were setting up a situation where one division or group of people might gain control over all of them and subsequently have undue power over everyone else, since everyone needed to use the materials. Joe may have seen his colleagues as stingy, foolish, or simply inefficient, because he didn't understand the importance of those materials in developing guanxi and maintaining a balance of power among the departments.

5. Not a good answer. Chinese companies are no different from American companies in that there is both cooperation and competition among departments for skilled personnel, scarce resources, the attention of the leadership, and so forth. Controlling access to information is an important way that divisions within an organization acquire and maintain power. Try to find an answer that better addresses this issue.

14 Got a Match?

1. This is a good answer. Many Chinese would point to the high American divorce rate as evidence of the fact that young people, and even not-so-young people, are not very good at

picking their own mates. In general, Chinese young people will consult with their parents and older relatives about whom to marry. Even when a Chinese youth has chosen his or her own partner, the approval of the parents is very important, and the marriage is unlikely to go forward until the parents and perhaps even other relatives on both sides have been persuaded of its suitability. If the parents pick a suitable spouse and if the child agrees that the match is a good one, everyone begins with the assumption that the relationship will be a good and lasting one. Even the most individualistic American would have to admit that such a positive attitude is a sound beginning for a marriage (Brislin 2000).

One of our Chinese authors is reminded of a former roommate (we'll call him Cao) who allowed his department chair to arrange a marriage for him after several years of unhappy experiences with blind dates set up by his friends and a number of other self-initiated relationships that didn't get off the ground. Cao's friends had introduced him to many beautiful women who were interested in a man with a Ph.D. and the potential to study or work abroad, but the women were cool and quiet and showed little interest in drawing the shy Cao out of his shell. The department chair was able to recognize qualities in Cao that his same-age peers could not, and the match was a success. We think this is because the department chair was able to take a broader view than Cao's younger, less-experienced friends (Kagitcibasi 1997). The older man took into account the families of the couple, their goals for their children, and their ability to get along as two families. He also considered the young couple's long-term goals, their personalities, and, perhaps most important, their shortcomings. The department chair found a woman who was beautiful and who valued Cao's education and potential to move overseas but who also was (a) too tall for most men but not for Cao and (b) lively and talkative and thus able to compensate for Cao's shyness. The woman who was "too tall" and the man who was "too shy" complemented each other well. Cao is one man who considers himself lucky that in China one can turn over the choice of a spouse to someone who is older and wiser.

2. On the contrary, most city-bred Chinese question and challenge the old traditions on a daily basis. Most young urban Chinese would have thoroughly considered whether to pick their own mate or leave the choice to their elders. Look for another alternative.

3. Not a good answer. Few Chinese, even in rural areas, cling to Confucianist thought to this degree. Most Chinese would probably maintain that a woman's obedience to her father, husband, and sons would indeed be inconsistent with success in a career and modern thinking. For most Chinese the decision to allow trusted elders to choose one's spouse is a reasoned choice, not unthinking traditional behavior. Look for a better explanation.

4. This is a good answer. Most urban Chinese youth who decide to let their parents choose their future partners are probably thinking along these lines. Shy, sober college students who watch their friends go through one broken heart and disillusionment after another in the dating game are likely to be among those who decide to let their parents make their decision for them.

    It's important to realize that in such matchmaking situations, the young people *do* have the right to say no. Also, independence from parents for its own sake is not as highly valued in Chinese culture as it is in the more individualistic U.S. culture. In fact, dependence on parents and other elders and authority figures is encouraged and approved of in Chinese culture, where most individuals are comparatively comfortable with hierarchical relationships.

15 Is More Expected of Leaders?

1. This, admittedly, is a difficult incident, and the interpretation of several alternatives hinges on the guidance in one culture compared with the other. In this incident, we are arguing that Greg's urban American culture does not give explicit guidance about considering the personal morality of leaders. Rather, in the United States this is a personal issue. It is up to individuals to make judgments about a person's leadership skills and about his or her morality. At times, Americans will conclude that although personal morality

could be at a higher level, they are willing to set that aside when thinking about potential leaders. Remember that members of the American voting public were willing to set aside their opinions about President Clinton's extramarital affairs. Even when it was proven that he had had a sexual relationship with a young White House intern and then lied about it to a grand jury, citizens seemed more impressed by near-zero inflation and low unemployment than upset about the president's immorality. A similar case could be made about President John Kennedy. Many knew about his extramarital affairs, but they were willing to set this aside when considering his leadership. We are quite willing to point out, on the other hand, that this explanation will not be accurate for all parts of the United States or for all groups of Americans. This is not a good answer. Please choose again.

2. This is a good answer. We have drawn the following conclusions about leadership from a number of sources (Earley 1997; Hu and Grove 1999; Hui 1990; Ling 1989; C. J. Zhu 1999). In China there are three concepts that people keep in mind when thinking about leaders. The first is the ability of leaders to deal with the workload assigned to them, and the second is their ability to deal effectively with the social needs of their subordinates (motivation, morale, integration of individuals into cooperative work groups, etc.). These two, incidentally, are also concepts Americans use when thinking about leaders in the workplace. The third concept is more a part of people's thinking in China than in the United States, and this third concept involves the personal morality of leaders. Leaders should behave according to high moral standards, and having a romantic relationship with a secretary is not considered exemplary of high morals. Reasons include the fact that the secretary may be favored by the Chinese boss and that the relation has become sexual outside any marital bond (frowned upon in China more than in urban areas in the United States). Keep in mind that Chinese coworkers, more than Greg, would be able to pick up subtle cues that indicate preferential treatment in the workplace and the probability of a sexual relationship. If a similar incident took place among Americans in Boston, Greg more than Lao Zhang would be able to perceive subtle cues in-

dicative of preferential treatment or a sexual relationship. In the incident, then, Lao Zhang has become a "poor" leader due to people's suspicions about the possible sexual relationship and so has a difficult time marshaling the support of subordinates and peers.

One of us offered this Chinese perspective: Chinese history is full of heroes and leaders. They are held up to the Chinese, from childhood, as role models, but they are more than just role models; they are idolized. Sometimes their moral virtues are more important than their actual leadership qualities. Confusing relationships with female employees are something Chinese leaders particularly want to avoid. A person's leadership qualities will immediately be called into question once people find out about any relationship with a female subordinate. As in the United States, however, different parts of the country are more or less conservative. As Western ideas flood into the country, people in more cosmopolitan areas, like Shanghai, are becoming more liberal about this kind of issue. Some people may begin to feel that a business leader's (if not a political leader's) personal and public lives might be separable. We are not saying that the Chinese do not have romantic relationships outside of marriage. Such relationships, however, are far more culturally acceptable if the people involved work in different organizations and if the relationships are carried on in a discreet manner. There is a saying in China that translates roughly as "The wise rabbit does not eat the grass that immediately surrounds it."

There is another answer that also helps with the interpretation of this incident, and we recommend that you look for it.

3. This is a good answer. As a generalization, people from highly individualistic cultures such as the United States make a sharp distinction between what they consider "people's private business" and what they consider appropriate public knowledge about themselves. In this incident, Greg remembered that his relationship with a female subordinate (who eventually became his second wife) was considered his own business and nobody else's. He is likely to interpret the incident

involving Lao Zhang from this frame of mind and conclude that Lao Zhang's relationship with a secretary should not be considered public knowledge. In China, there is not so sharp a distinction between "my own business" and "other people's business." People take great interest in the lives of others, and membership in a collective is marked by a great deal of shared knowledge of matters that would be considered private in an individualistic culture. Good advice for individualists moving to a collectivistic culture is to practice giving more personal information about themselves during interactions with collectivists. Another piece of intercultural wisdom is that when collectivists start revealing personal information about themselves and clearly expect sojourning individualists to provide similar information, this is an indicator that the sojourners are being accepted as welcomed visitors, rather than mere intruders, to the culture.

4. There is not as sharp a distinction between "my own personal business" and "things about me that are known to others" in China compared with the United States, and so this is not a good answer. Co-workers would not feel that they are "nosy" or that they are "busybodies" just because they talk frequently about Lao Zhang and his relationship with the secretary. Such a relationship is appropriate knowledge to be considered part of public discourse. Please choose again.

5. Choosing this alternative may indicate that you are on the right track, but there are better answers. In China, people do form romantic relationships after meeting members of the opposite sex in their organization. However, such relationships are considered much more appropriate (a) if the man and woman are unmarried and have no current romantic attachment with anyone else, (b) if they are from very different branches of a large organization such that one person does not have a supervisory relation with the other, and (c) if the supervisors of both people have signaled acceptance of the romantic relationship. In this incident, Lao Zhang had a romantic and possibly a sexual relationship with a subordinate, behavior that was not considered appropriate. Please choose again.

Part Five

The Workplace: Motivations

16 Fair Price?

Ken Kopp, an American importer, successfully negotiated a contract with Zhen Jian Garment Factory in southern Jiangsu Province to purchase forty-six thousand winter coats in three months. The first two months went very smoothly. Ken was satisfied with everything, from quality control to prompt shipping; he was even more surprised with the speed of production. One summer afternoon he decided to drive down from his headquarters in a large hotel in a nearby city to inspect some of the factory's workshops. He was pleased to find himself cordially greeted by every worker he met. Through his interpreter he readily told some inquisitive Chinese workers that he was paying their company ten dollars for each coat, which he would then sell for two hundred dollars in the United States. The following week the American manager unexpectedly noticed a sharp decline in the quality of the garments at the packing department. He immediately raised his concern with the Chinese manager and tightened quality inspection. Nothing seemed to help. The pile of rejected coats just kept growing to the point that it was impossible to finish the contract in time.

What went wrong?

1. Forty-six thousand garments in three months was simply too much for a normal Chinese manufacturer. Mr. Kopp was unrealistically ambitious to expect trouble-free business with the Chinese. He should have started with small contracts to learn about the business environment before tackling larger projects.

2. Mr. Kopp shouldn't have visited the workshops, since the Chinese make a clear distinction between someone "in the group"

and someone "outside the group." By going there, Mr. Kopp broke the code of conduct that determined his relationship with the workers, who in turn turned out shoddy garments to punish the outsider.

3. Mr. Kopp shouldn't have revealed the selling price of the garment. By doing so he suggested to the Chinese workers that he was making a huge profit, which the workers perceived as Western exploitation.

4. Chinese workers are very accustomed to hierarchical company structure in which they readily take orders and demands from serious and authoritative managers. Once they found out that Mr. Kopp was so easygoing, they felt the pressure to work hard had been removed and assumed that he might well forgive mistakes in their work.

Explanations for Fair Price? begin on page 127.

17   What Motivates Chinese Employees?

Robert McMahon was excited about the new venture in Dalian. With its low labor costs and rapid economic growth, China offered great prospects for the business. His company had decided to enter China as a wholly owned subsidiary of the parent telecommunications firm. Robert knew a few of the government officials in Dalian, as his company had previously exported its goods to China through the city. The company knew the venture was risky, but due to its relations with officials in Dalian, it felt the investment would be successful. Robert, it was agreed, would take the lead in management.

Robert was fairly confident in his abilities as a manager and his expertise in international business. He had also spent several recent years at the company's Asia-Pacific regional headquarters, working on exporting goods to China. He therefore kept abreast of the developing political and economic situation there. He was assertive and prided himself on being able to stay on top of things.

To start off, Robert felt it was important, despite the low labor costs, to allow for material incentives such as bonuses. He was sure the workers within the subsidiary, most of whom were Chinese, would respond wholeheartedly to his incentive scheme. He was particularly generous to the middle managers, offering monetary incentives for improved performance. He certainly had had success before with such incentive programs.

As the initial months passed, Robert sensed that things were not progressing as he had planned. Some of the workers seemed to be doing well and working hard, but many managers and several workers did not seem to be responding as enthusiastically to the bonuses as Robert had expected. He was a little confused.

What cultural aspects as applied to the Chinese business environment help explain Robert's confusion?

1. The fact that the managers were receiving "particularly generous" monetary incentives was at odds with Chinese egalitarianism.

2. Robert had not developed a proper relationship with the managers. The incentive scheme had nothing to do with the problem.

3. Chinese workers do not respond well to foreign leadership.

4. Chinese workers and managers need other incentives beyond just material rewards or compensation.

5. Chinese workers take more time to accomplish tasks due to their tendency to socialize as groups.

Explanations for What Motivates Chinese Employees? begin on page 128.

18   The Entrepreneur

Chad Peterson was excited about his new promotion and transfer—to China! He had served well in the marketing department of his company and had been promoted to assist the director of marketing at the company's recently established operations in Guangzhou. Chad had studied a bit about the Chinese, but he had worked thus far in the United States and had little experience with Chinese individuals or culture. Because he had about two months before relocating, Chad frequented the local university library in an attempt to absorb all he could about China, its culture, and its way of doing business. In addition, his company provided a week-long cultural orientation seminar just prior to his departure.

After arriving in Guangzhou, Chad found that the work was exciting and that marketing to the Chinese was a new challenge. During his orientation seminar, he had learned several concepts that were important in the Chinese business environment, among them *guanxi* (connections) and Confucian dynamism. He had also learned about individualism and collectivism and that China tended to be collectivistic while his own culture, the United States, ranked high on individualism. He felt he had a basic understanding of these concepts and was sure he would learn more.

Because the marketing director had two assistants, Chad worked closely with Feng Dashan, his Chinese counterpart. Chad learned that Feng came from a fairly influential family in the area and was highly motivated and worked very hard. To Chad it seemed that Feng Dashan was quite "individualistic" in his behavior. He worked diligently for bonuses, was always going the extra mile, and had set a number of work-related goals for himself.

After a few months, Feng Dashan left the company to start a venture of his own. Chad kept in touch with Feng and heard from others that his new business was doing well. One weekend Feng Dashan invited Chad to dinner at his home. Many of Feng's relatives were present as well as some friends whom Chad had not met. Chad found Feng Dashan's house quite nice and equipped with all the latest big-ticket consumer items such as a big-screen TV, a VCD (video compact disk) player, modern kitchen appliances, a laptop computer, and so forth. Chad also learned that Feng had recently purchased a new car for his parents. Later, after speaking with him, Chad understood that Feng Dashan's business was very profitable and successful. He was managing it himself and already had some forty to fifty employees. It seemed to Chad that Feng Dashan was doing quite a good job of being individualistic.

Were all those cultural lessons wrong? Help Chad understand.

1. Collectivism is simply related to money. When a person has more money, he or she will be more individualistic.

2. Feng Dashan is an exception to the general description of the Chinese being collectivists.

3. Chad doesn't understand the subtleties of individualism and collectivism. Feng Dashan is not necessarily an individualist.

4. Individualism and collectivism are concepts of decreasing importance in a world of increased economic integration.

5. Chad needs to review his lessons on Confucian dynamism, the Neo-Confucian philosophy that deals with economic issues prevalent among the Asian economies.

Explanations for The Entrepreneur begin on page 132.

19   In the Eyes of Whom?

"I chose to join the Bradshaw Construction Company because of its forward-looking policies," Jeff Monahan told Chu Jin on the way to town from the airport. The executives at Bradshaw had asked Chu Jin, from Beijing, to spend about six months with the company in the hopes of eventually developing joint ventures in large construction projects in China. Jeff was aware that Bradshaw was borrowing a page from the postwar "Japanese economic miracle." Many companies had developed successful ventures in Japan by first integrating Japanese managers into activities at the U.S. headquarters. Given their newly developed familiarity with American business practices and their new networks, the Japanese managers had been in a good position to speak favorably about the American companies once they had returned to Japan. Bradshaw was hoping the same strategy would pay off with the Chinese. In addition to hosting Chu Jin in Boston, Bradshaw Construction had sent one of its engineers, Mark Todd, to live for ten months in the northern Chinese city where Chu Jin's company had its headquarters.

Jeff and Chu Jin hit it off quickly. They each had an interest in playing competitive bridge, and both had the ranking of senior master. They played as partners and did well in local tournaments. Given this mutual interest, they developed a good relationship and felt comfortable sharing their candid thoughts.

Chu Jin learned that Bradshaw had recently donated large amounts of money to the reelection campaigns of several prominent politicians. Wanting to learn about the wide range of American business practices, he asked Jeff to explain this expenditure of money. Jeff replied that since Bradshaw had donated generously to campaign funds, the company would be looked upon more favorably when there were government construction projects on which the company might bid. "That seems corrupt to me," Chu Jin replied. "Aren't you using money to buy influence with politicians?"

"This is the way things are!" Jeff replied. "You can't be naive about such things and hope to survive in the construction business. And what's all this about corruption anyway? Our representative in China, Mark Todd, e-mailed me recently that he had to grease the palm of a so-called civil servant to get his driver's license without waiting forever. If that's not corruption, what is?"

Of the following statements, one or more summarizes reasonable generalizations that might be offered to Chu Jin and Jeff.

1. American businesspeople are more sensitive to charges that aspects of business practice are corrupt than are Chinese businesspeople.

2. Chinese businesspeople are more sensitive to charges that aspects of business practice are corrupt than are American businesspeople.

3. People in various cultures are accustomed to living with business practices that sojourners from other countries might label as corrupt.

4. In all likelihood, neither Jeff nor Chu Jin was comfortable with the business practices that were pointed out in this incident by the outsider to their culture.

Explanations for In the Eyes of Whom? begin on page 135.

20   VCD Players for China

Bud was excited about his promotion and the new possibilities associated with his position. He had recently worked for several months on developing a business plan for entering markets in mainland China and had also been careful to maintain and increase his contacts there. Bud's company felt it was time to enter the Chinese market and selected Bud to take the lead, operating out of Hong Kong, where the company maintained a regional headquarters for its Asia operations. Bud would report directly to the regional vice president.

After some research, Bud felt that the company, which produced consumer electronic devices, would do best in China by first introducing its video compact disc (VCD) players due to the increasing popularity of VCDs among the growing middle class. The company could then introduce its televisions, building upon lessons learned from introducing the VCD players.

Because of his contacts in several major cities within China, Bud was successful in securing the necessary permits and developing distribution channels for the VCD players. The last hurdle was implementing a good marketing plan. Bud had specialized in marketing during business school and had done well with a firm marketing cameras in the United States. He wanted to make a great hit with the initial entry of the product, and to do so, he decided to emphasize the image or lifestyle association he knew a VCD player would bring to its proud owner. He would also introduce the company's "loaded" model, which had plenty of gadgets and all the extras. Finally, in conjunction with the image emphasis, Bud decided to introduce the product with a great promotional offer. Individuals purchasing the product within ninety days of its introduction would receive their choice of either a classy T-shirt with the company logo or a pair of sunglasses with the company logo on the frames. Additionally, buyers would receive their choice of one of ten Western VCDs free of charge.

Bud worked out the final details and, with a prayer, launched the product. Despite what he thought was a great marketing plan, Bud was disappointed with the first month's sales. In fact, the product did miserably.

As a culturally informed business consultant, what advice could you offer Bud?

1. Bud failed by focusing on the image or lifestyle association of the product. The Chinese are more interested in the details of a product.

2. The Chinese are wary of Western imports and prefer to buy local brands.

3. The VCD player, and particularly the "loaded" model, had too many gadgets. The Chinese aren't interested in all the fancy extras; they prefer simple products.

4. The product had not been in the market long enough. The security that a well-known brand affords is important to the Chinese.

5. Bud failed by promoting the product too strongly. The Chinese feel that a good product does not need excessive promotion.

Explanations for VCD Players for China begin on page 137.

21   The Incentive Program

Doug Godar, a successful businessperson from Boston, was given wide latitude regarding decision making by his company's representatives back home in the head office. In Shanghai, he was able to develop a promising line of casual women's wear in collaboration with executives from a large Chinese manufacturing firm. While satisfied with the performance of about twenty midlevel managers, Doug felt that an incentive program might spur production. He began a set of meetings with managers in various offices, some of whom he had only occasionally visited in the past, since these managers were capably supervised by Chinese executives. After these meetings, he decided to introduce the type of incentive program that had worked well for him in the United States.

Doug announced that managers who demonstrated increased production within their units would be eligible for participation in a travel-study program that would take them to Europe and to the United States. When asked the reasonable question, "How many such travel opportunities would there be?" he responded by saying that there was no limit. If managers demonstrated increased productivity, they would be eligible for the travel opportunity.

After about six months, Doug reviewed production figures and found that the manager of one unit, Wen Yan Rong, had been especially effective. Doug thought that giving Wen the first travel award would be a good idea and would serve a number of functions: it would recognize Wen's hard work; it would make clear to others that the travel awards were indeed a reality and not a vague promise; and it would also give other managers a goal to work toward, since they could look at Wen's production figures and set corresponding ambitious targets for themselves.

However, after Doug made the announcement about the first award, the other managers did not seem to work harder so that they might receive the travel opportunity. Doug also heard that there was a lot of grumbling about the entire incentive program.

If Doug asked you for your reactions, what would you say to help him understand this incident?

1.   International travel opportunities are not a highly valued incentive among Chinese managers.

2.   Many of the Chinese managers may have believed that if one person receives an award, there is less likelihood that anyone else will receive one.

3. The Chinese do not have experience with statistics such that they can monitor unit productivity in the manner favored by Doug.

4. Programs designed to increase productivity that work well in the United States do not travel well to China.

Explanations for The Incentive Program begin on page 139.

22   Whose Ideas Are These?

John Coleman was twenty-five and an ambitious businessman. He had recently graduated with an MBA degree from a prestigious American university. From the age of eighteen he had been interested in China and had become convinced that this extremely large country represented great potential for international investments. During his college years he had studied Chinese and become reasonably fluent.

After being hired by an American pharmaceutical company, John convinced his superiors that the company would be well served if he were assigned to China. One of John's superiors happened to know of some Chinese businesspeople who wanted to look into the possibilities of expanding their line of nonprescription medicines. This superior contacted the Chinese businesspeople, and they agreed to work with John out of their offices in Shanghai.

After arriving in Shanghai and settling in, John reported to work. He discovered that his supervisor in China would be Fang Da-chun, a fifty-year-old businessman who had recently been able to amass considerable wealth working with American firms desirous of expansion in China. Mr. Fang was impressed with John's Chinese skills and immediately began including him in meetings with other Chinese. Grateful for this attention, John shared some of his ideas for the manufacturing of nonprescription drugs.

One afternoon Mr. Fang invited John to a meeting with the executives of a Chinese pharmaceutical company. Mr. Fang presented some ideas about possible future joint ventures between himself and this company. John was pleased to hear Mr. Fang present some of John's own ideas, but he was not pleased after the meeting when he realized that Mr. Fang never made a connection between the ideas and the person who had originally developed them. John concluded that he could not work with Mr. Fang, and he began to consider drafting a letter to his company in the United States recommending the severing of ties with Mr. Fang.

If John asked your advice concerning whether he should send a letter to his American company, what might you tell him?

1. In Chinese, the syntactic form that indicates the relationship between an abstract concept (e.g., a person's idea) and the person responsible for the concept is difficult. You might suggest that John may not have learned this grammatical form, even in advanced studies of Chinese language in the United States.

2. You might tell John that he has encountered a problem common in China: people take ideas with no thought of giving anything in return.

3. Mr. Fang feels that since he is looking after John for his business acquaintance in America, he should be compensated in some way, such as being able to use John's ideas. Tell John this.

4. You might explain to John that Mr. Fang is likely to show his gratitude in ways other than mentioning John's name during the meeting with the Chinese pharmaceutical executives.

5. You know that John feels that his ideas have been stolen from him. You are also aware that Mr. Fang feels that John's ideas have become part of shared knowledge and that there no longer has to be an explicit link made between the idea and its originator. Inform John of this.

Explanations for Whose Ideas Are These? begin on page 141.

Explanations for the Incidents in Part Five

16 Fair Price?

1. This may be true in general, but it is not a sufficient explanation for the situation in question. Chinese companies have been known to agree to contracts that promise more than they can deliver, simply to land a contract or because they *hope* that they can meet the production deadlines. However, in this case, the factory had been producing the product on schedule for two months. There is no reason to believe that they were suddenly unable to do so.

2. This is not a good answer. Chinese culture is not so different from American culture that inspecting the factory that is putting out one's product is strange or inappropriate. On the contrary, if an importer never visited the shop floor, the workers might suspect that he didn't care what they did, and quality might suffer.

3. This is the most likely explanation. Westerners and Chinese perceive profit differently. Free enterprise is a relatively new concept to many mainland Chinese workers, and the difference between what their company was paid and the final price of the product horrified them. They were unlikely to understand that in addition to paying their factory for the production of the garments, Mr. Kopp's company needed to pay for the materials used in the garments, shipping to the United States, advertising, and so on. For very good historical reasons, the Chinese fear exploitation at the hands of Western capitalists, and they are suspicious when Western investors make profits, even though they know that is why they have come to China in the first place (Gao 1993; Tomlinson 1999). The workers in this incident were completely demoralized to learn that the garments they were making were being sold for a sum equivalent to several months' salary for each of them. Ken was unwise to assume that Chinese factory workers would understand the other expenses involved in import trade. The workers undoubtedly felt that they were being taken advantage of, and the quality of their work suffered as a result. Without realizing

it, Mr. Kopp also intimated the difference in wealth between the United States and China by indirectly suggesting that many Americans would be able to afford the coats.

How could Ken have answered the workers' question without getting himself into trouble? Of course he could have refused to answer at all, but that might have aroused the workers' suspicions. He could have saved the workers' face—and gotten his coats on schedule—if he had answered with Chinese indirection, "I think Americans will be willing to pay a lot for these well-made coats." This answer, while true, compliments the workers while avoiding anything specific which would give them cause to feel taken advantage of.

4. It's true that Chinese workers are accustomed to a hierarchical company structure and to taking orders and meeting the demands of authoritative managers. However, this is not a hard-and-fast rule, and an authoritarian manner is not by any means considered an indispensable quality in a Chinese manager. In addition, there is no indication that Mr. Kopp's friendly manner was relevant to the present discussion. Chinese people expect foreigners to be different from them, and they would not be likely to take an American visitor's jovial attitude on the factory floor as indication that he or she did not expect to continue receiving high quality goods. There is a better answer.

17   What Motivates Chinese Employees?

1. Not a bad guess. One of the American authors offered this perspective: the Chinese have traditionally sought harmony within groups (Pye 1982). One aspect of this harmony is equality and sharing among group members. The concept of egalitarianism in society was emphasized with the advent of Chinese Communism under the leadership of Mao Zedong. Recently, however, with economic reform and the disparity in economic development in the coastal versus inland provinces, the difference in income between rich and poor in China is continuing to grow. The governmental response to this is to tolerate a degree of inequality for now as the country as a whole moves toward economic prosperity.

The fact that the managers received a generous bonus might not have been such a sensitive issue in the current period of reform. Whether or not this was a problem would depend on the structure of the subsidiary, the types of groups that may have evolved, and the role managers played in those groups.

One of the Chinese authors offered a different perspective: before economic reform, Chinese workers all belonged to a unit, or work· group. The managers were considered role models within these units. They were expected to take care of the welfare of the workers before considering their own needs. This could be one reason that the particularly generous bonuses did not motivate the managers very well. They may not have been ready to move out of the role that they had been playing for decades. This raises a more important issue: what type of reward for good work might these managers be more accustomed to and willing to accept? Look for an alternative that explains this.

2. While it is important to develop the proper relationship with subordinate managers, this incident does not provide enough background on the development of relationships between Robert and the middle managers to support this answer. There is a better answer, which involves cultural factors and the incentive scheme.

3. This is an inaccurate generalization. How Chinese workers respond to foreign leadership depends to a great extent upon the individual personality of the person in that role. If a particular individual is sensitive to Chinese culture in the workplace, he or she may be very well received. It is also clear that foreign managers who are unwilling to understand cultural issues or who are careless in their approach to working with Chinese workers and managers will be received rather poorly.

With the "open-door" policy, foreign investment has flooded into China. Westerners have set up representative offices, joint ventures, wholly owned subsidiaries, and other forms of investment; they have created a lot of employment opportunities for the Chinese people. Foreign organizations usually pay their employees much better than local firms do, and they purportedly give female employees more opportunities to develop their talents. Usually it is considered a privilege to work under foreign leaders. If the Chinese are not responding well to a particular foreign leader, it is personal management style, rather than nationality, that is likely to be the problem.

Another important point is that workers in foreign firms have to apply for employment; in other words, they must want to work for a foreign company and under foreign leadership.

4. This is the best answer. A number of studies (Choi, Nisbett, and Norenzayan 1999) have been conducted regarding the influence of cultural background on motivation schemes. There is empirical evidence showing that monetary incentives work better in individualistic cultures than in collectivistic cultures. People have different kinds of needs: (a) physiological needs such as food, drink, and health; (b) physical safety and emotional security, for example, adequate clothing, shelter, and protection against attack (including unemployment benefits, redundancy pay, and old-age pensions); (c) affection, needs like belonging to mutually supportive groups such as family units, small work groups, and so on; (d) esteem, self-respect, and feelings of accomplishment for achievements, which must be recognized and appreciated by someone else; and (e) self-fulfillment, utilizing one's potential to the maximum by working with and for one's fellow beings (Maslow 1970).

    Chinese workers have only recently been able to satisfy their survival and safety needs. What they need is affection and the sense of belonging. Therefore, sometimes nonmonetary rewards such as recognition of good performance or training and development opportunities work better than purely financial incentives.

    Another perspective comes from the literature that focuses on studies that are specific to China: recent studies about work motivation and reward-systems design have revealed important characteristics of the Chinese workforce (Hui 1990; Dorfman 1996; C. J. Zhu 1999). In the early 1980s several research projects in Chinese enterprises found that social needs were most important to employees. Factory workers in northern China ranked social needs (such as contributions to their own organizations and the country's modernization) highest, although material incentives were identified as important as well. Age differences and organizational position affected the kinds of rewards employees preferred. Young employees preferred technical training and having clean, comfortable, prestigious jobs. Middle-aged employees felt that bonuses were more important. For the older employees, social rewards (such as an impressive work title) appeared to be more important. There are three important implications from these studies. First, various reward programs should be designed to meet the needs of employees who are of different ages and who have different jobs and organizational positions. Second, many employees feel the intrinsic rewards, such as technical training, a satisfying job, and the opportunity to go abroad for training or business, are more important than material rewards. Third, a flexible and comprehensive multiple-rewards structure combining social rewards with material incentives is most effective at motivating the Chinese workforce.

Robert simply applied a material incentive scheme, which works rather well in the West. If he had combined material incentives with social and intrinsic rewards (depending on age and position), his approach for motivating Chinese workers and managers would have been more successful.

One of our Chinese authors comments: a one-time payment, such as a bonus, may not give the employee the sense of security that he or she values. A worker wants to know that the money is going to continue to come in. However, this author also feels that monetary incentives are catching on rapidly in the wake of economic changes. Over the past decade, one has begun to hear average Chinese workers say "*You qian hao ban shi*," which means "If you give me money (i.e., pay me enough), I'll work for you." A pun that is in common current usage illustrates this. "*Xiang qian kan*" can mean either "looking at the money" or "looking forward into the future." The implication, of course, is that looking at the money *is* looking to the future.

Obviously the issue of how best to motivate Chinese workers is not a simple one, and the wise manager will consider his or her own situation in light of these somewhat disparate observations on Chinese culture.

5. This is not an accurate generalization about Chinese workers. There is no evidence showing that Chinese workers spend too much time socializing or that they are less efficient than workers in other countries. In fact, there is evidence (e.g., Earley's 1989 study on social loafing and collectivism) that Chinese people are more productive when working under conditions of shared responsibility than in conditions of individuality. Finally, there is nothing in this incident to suggest that these workers are socializing too much.

18   The Entrepreneur

1. This is too simple an explanation to be valid. Having money may allow a person more avenues by which to express individuality and pursue personal goals. Just as important, however, having money may allow a person greater avenues by which to benefit a particular group or collective. Thus, it could be assumed that a collectivist might have every bit as much motivation to amass wealth as an individualist; it would be only their goals—the benefit of the collective as opposed to personal gain—that would be different. Interestingly, this assumption may be less true than in former times. In 1970 Geert Hofstede found a .82 correlation between individualism and a country's gross national product (GNP) per capita. With 1980 data the figure was still high (.71) (Hofstede 1980) but had dropped. This suggests that perhaps over the long run, a country's increasing wealth may influence the degree of individualistic behavior; the results in the short term, however, are not well established. Many countries of East and Southeast Asia (e.g., South Korea, Taiwan, Singapore, Hong Kong) have experienced rapid economic growth in recent decades. Still, these countries must be considered collectivist in nature. The relationship between wealth and individualism/collectivism is not clear, but we surely cannot assume that collectivism is inimical to economic growth and development (Kagitcibasi 1997).

2. This is not a good answer. Feng Dashan most certainly is a collectivist. His purchase of a new car for his parents and his success at rapidly developing a new business, which implies good guanxi networks, are clues suggesting that Feng Dashan

is a collectivist. In fact, his success as a businessman is as likely due to the guanxi network of his well-connected extended family as it is to any particular entrepreneurial skill he may possess.

3. This is the best answer. Feng Dashan's behavior indicates that he is very much a collectivist. How many Americans (individualists) buy their parents a car with their new wealth? When Chad visits, the house is full of Feng Dashan's relatives. A person from an individualistic culture like Chad's might not assume that the relatives visit much more often than he himself does, but a collectivist like Feng Dashan would know that they are likely to be there very often indeed.

   In a collectivist culture, when an individual in the collective does well, the whole collective benefits: parents, relatives, and even close family friends (Bhawuk 1998). When Feng Dashan "goes the extra mile," works hard for bonuses, and sets work-related goals for himself—behaviors that Chad interprets as individualistic—he is doing so not only for himself, but also to bring a good name, prosperity, and comfort to his extended family and those they are close to. Feng Dashan's business success, when he sets off on his own, is not his success alone; it is shared by his entire collective. And, since Feng Dashan is such a dedicated collectivist, his employees are probably also experiencing a better life, since a good collectivistic boss takes care of his or her workers.

   Chad may be confusing a desire for success and personal achievement with individualism. In his mind, he may see Feng as "the winner" and his competitors in business as losing out. Perhaps it does not occur to Chad to think about how Feng Dashan's success is also success for his family, friends, and even his workers and his neighbors, since an individualistic American like himself would not be likely to consider sharing such a large portion of the fruits of his own hard work with his family members and others.

4. Although there is some truth in this answer, there are other, better alternatives. It is true that the traditional distinction between individualism and collectivism is blurred in a world of economic integration. In business settings, individualism

and collectivism may be less important than market forces. Particularly in a setting where collectivists and individualists work in close cooperation, such as in the increasingly numerous Sino-American joint-venture companies, company policies and rules, corporate culture, and the necessity of cooperation to achieve shared goals and objectives may supersede cultural conditioning to individualism and collectivism. Nevertheless, individualism and collectivism comprise one of the major dimensions of cross-cultural differences. This difference is not going to disappear or become insignificant any time soon.

5. This is a good answer. Confucian dynamism offers another perspective from which to examine Feng Dashan's behavior. *Confucian dynamism*, or *Neo-Confucianism*, is the term for a cultural dimension found to be distinct from Hofstede's four dimensions (individualism/collectivism, power distance, masculinity/femininity, and uncertainty avoidance) and prevalent among East Asian nations (1980). Michael Bond headed a team of researchers dubbed the "Chinese Culture Connection" to develop a survey instrument from a Chinese perspective. They published their results in 1987. Later, Bond worked with Hofstede to refine the dimension (Hofstede, Bond 1988). Interestingly, many of the teachings of Confucius could readily be identified in the set of values associated with the newly discovered dimension— hence the name Confucian dynamism. Confucian dynamism emphasizes the Confucian values of persistence and perseverance, ordering relationships by status and observing this order, thrift, and a sense of shame. Conversely, personal steadiness and stability, protecting face, respect for tradition, and the reciprocation of greetings, favors, and gifts receive relatively less emphasis. The Asian countries that have experienced rapid growth in recent decades—Japan, South Korea, Taiwan, Hong Kong, and Singapore—tend to emphasize those certain aspects of Confucian thinking and give other aspects relatively less emphasis. Inherent in the concept are a focus on "the future" and "hard work," not concepts normally associated with Confucian teachings.

What does all this mean for Feng Dashan? On the job, Chad noticed that Feng was persistent and persevering, or, as he put it, "always going the extra mile." He was future-oriented and worked in Chad's firm to gain experience in the hope of later developing his own business, which he now has. He appears to have a clear ordering of relationships. He honors and observes the status of his parents. Confucian dynamism would seem to be a possible explanation for Feng Dashan's behavior and Chad's confusion. There is, however, an even better explanation. Look for another alternative.

19   In the Eyes of Whom?

1. The developers of this incident are not convinced that this is true. It is certainly not true of the Americans and Chinese that we know. The businesspeople we know seem about equally thin- or thick-skinned when discussions about corruption in business practices arise. What may be true is that there are different business practices in each culture, and some of these may seem corrupt to outsiders (Francesco and Gold 1998). Sometimes (not always!) explanations of the business practices help put them in perspective and help outsiders to understand the practices from the host's viewpoint (e.g., see Textbooks for All, page 208). But to complicate the picture, thoughtful people from most cultures often admit that they wish some practices were different and did not put some individuals (e.g., those unwilling to put up money for favors) at a disadvantage. Please choose again.

2. While this might be a commonly heard stereotype, we know of no evidence that Chinese businesspeople are either more or less sensitive to charges of corrupt business practices. We explained our position in our suggested explanation for alternative 1.

3. This is a good answer. People are accustomed to certain facts about the business world in their country and do not think very much about them (Cushner and Brislin 1996) unless confronted by a thoughtful outsider, either from another culture or another profession quite different from that of the businessperson. As in this incident, many Americans are accustomed to requests to donate money to political campaigns. They may offer an explanation like the following: "It costs a lot of money to run a campaign, especially to buy

television time. American taxpayers have decided that they do not want the government to fund such campaigns, as is done in many European countries. Unless they have incredible individual wealth, how are people supposed to run their campaigns? Others have to donate money to see that their candidates get elected. But once they are elected, it is reasonable to expect that the politicians will look out for those that helped them get into office. They will want to reward their friends, as long as the friends (e.g., construction companies desiring government contracts) are capable of getting the work done. Who are the politicians supposed to reward? Their enemies?!"

What explanation might be offered for the example of corrupt behavior suggested for China? Chu Jin might suggest the following: "My guess is that Mark Todd thought that he could get his driver's license right away, within a few days at most. In China, however, bureaucracies move slowly and the clerks are overworked. If Mark Todd had been willing to wait the normal three months or so, like all Chinese have to do, then he would not have had to pay anything. But since he wanted special service, perhaps requiring a clerk to work beyond normal hours, he was expected to pay some money. Incidentally, an individual Chinese person in a hurry would also be expected to pay."

In addition to this alternative, there is another good choice.

4. We believe that this alternative captures a fact about human behavior, and we feel that it is a good choice. People are often unhappy with aspects of their culture but have learned to live with them. In the two examples of questionable business practices in the incident, Jeff is probably not happy about the necessity for political contributions, but he has learned to live with the system that requires them. Chu Jin is probably not happy with complex bureaucracies necessitating delays in seemingly routine tasks, but he is accustomed to them. Sometimes, people's negative reaction to practices in other cultures is not the recognition of problems, but rather ignorance of ways of coping with and/or working around the problems (Brake, Walker, and Walker 1995). Bureaucra-

cies can be frustrating in the United States, also, but many Americans know ways of working around them. For example, they might contact someone in the bureaucracy with whom they have a personal relationship and ask that person for help in "cutting through red tape." As another example, Americans wanting publicity for a community-service event are often dismayed, after carefully explaining the event to newspaper reporters, at the number of inaccuracies once the "information" is printed. These Americans often learn that it is best to learn how journalists write stories and to provide written press releases giving accurate information that the reporters can use with few or no modifications.

In addition to this alternative, there is another good choice. Please make another selection.

20 VCD Players for China

1. You are on the right track with this answer. It is true, in general, that the Chinese are very interested in learning the details of a product they plan to buy. They are comparison shoppers extraordinaire. They want to know the differences between several models by different firms, the benefits, costs, and special features before they buy. Then they will compare several individual units of the same model. In marketing the product, Bud would have done well to emphasize the competitive features of his company's VCD player and to focus on the information the Chinese desire for comparative shopping.

One reason for this attention to detail is that, with few exceptions, all sales are final in China. If Americans are dissatisfied with a product that they have bought, in the vast majority of cases they can return the product for a complete refund or at least an exchange. In China, even if an item is defective, it can be difficult, or even impossible, to return it. Attention to detail is imperative before the purchase, unless a person wants to get stuck with useless, high-ticket merchandise.

It is not true, however, that the Chinese are uninterested in the status a product gives its owners (Lee and Lo 1993; Cateora and Graham 1999). Brand-name computers,

VCD players, high-quality cameras, and big refrigerators are some of the more recent icons of status. However, this desire for status products must not be confused with the Western emphasis on marketing an image or lifestyle association. The Chinese *are* very interested in being perceived as having a certain type of lifestyle, but that image comes from ownership of products of proven quality. This is one of two good answers. Look for another alternative that explores a different aspect of Chinese consumer culture.

2. On the contrary, most Chinese prefer Western imports over local brands. Western products are generally perceived to be of higher quality than Chinese-made products are, and because they are usually considerably more expensive, there is status associated with owning products that carry North American, Japanese, or European brand names. Even as the quality of locally made products improves, and in spite of the considerable price advantage, Chinese consumers trust Western brands to be of superior quality.

3. This is not a good answer. In fact, just the opposite is true. The Chinese are particularly attracted by the little gadgets and fancy extras, and, unlike their American counterparts, they often learn how to use every one of them. The gadgets add to the novelty and curiosity that are part of the Chinese desire for the Western products that economic prosperity has allowed them to purchase. It is important to remember, though, that the extras must be perceived as adding value to the product. While the Chinese prefer fancy gadgets, they are not at all interested in useless gimmicks and features that they (and their neighbors) do not consider useful in some way or another.

4. This is a good answer. While the Chinese look for a number of different things in a product (discussed elsewhere in these explanations), a proven track record for a product is important. Bud needs to remember that establishing faith, trust, and relationships is very important to the Chinese, and that takes time.

    As was mentioned in the explanation of alternative 1, sales are final in China. Purchasing a brand with a sound reputation reduces the likelihood that one will end up with an unsatisfactory product.

Word of mouth is an important factor in the establishment of brand security, but it takes time. The fact that the product is foreign would lend it some credibility from the start, at least until proven wrong, but few Chinese are going to take a chance on a brand they have never heard of. Most will wait until friends, neighbors, and co-workers have tried the product and found it satisfactory. Bud needs to be patient. His first month's sales are a poor indicator of the product's ultimate success or failure.

Look for another alternative that takes a different perspective.

5. The validation sample did not strongly support this alternative. Still, we feel that it deserves some consideration. Confucius taught that modesty is a virtue; a person who promotes himself or his products is suspect. Bud's product may have failed, at least in the short run, because he promoted it too strongly. The Chinese reaction to the T-shirts, sunglasses, and free videos is most likely to be "What is wrong with this product that they need to bribe people to buy it?" Many Chinese feel excessive promotion cheapens a product. A quality product does not need special marketing gimmicks to induce consumers to buy it. The product will speak for itself, and consumers will certainly find out about it (Gao 1993). Bud would be better off emphasizing the important and relevant features in a thorough advertising campaign, after which the consumers would then be the best promoters (assuming the product is acceptable).

21 The Incentive Program

1. This is not the best answer. Actually, the opposite of this statement is true. Chinese managers value international travel, and if they have the opportunity for such travel, they view it with great favor. Receipt of such travel opportunities is viewed as status-enhancing. Please choose again.

2. This is a good answer. As we have discussed several times, it is always difficult to make broad generalizations. There will undoubtedly be exceptions to any statement that includes generalizations that Chinese think this way and Americans

think that way. With this caveat, we believe that it is reasonable to suggest that many Chinese think in "win-lose" terms more frequently than do many Americans. In win-lose thinking, people believe that if something good happens to one person, there is less chance of something good happening to another person. In other words, the size of the pie is fixed, and if one person gets a big piece, there will be less for the others (Pruitt 1998). If person A receives a travel award or a raise or wins a lottery, there is less chance for something good to happen to person B. In this incident, then, other Chinese managers felt that since Wen Yan Rong had received the travel opportunity, the possibility that they might receive a similar benefit was reduced.

In contrast, people in some other cultures are more likely to think in terms of "win-win" situations, to believe that there is no limit to the number of good things that can happen to people (Fukuyama 1995). The pie is not limited in size. In fact, if something good happens to one person, it can be taken as a sign that there may be benefits for others as well. Often, people are happy when good things happen to another, since they may conclude that there are lots of benefits available if they work hard to obtain them. One of our American authors remembers a conversation with a professor during his graduate school years. The professor said, "It is in my personal interest to help a colleague obtain a research grant from a prestigious funding source, even if I don't see a penny of the money. If my colleague gets a grant, that becomes a signal to others that I work at an organization where people obtain funds from prestigious sources. That reputation helps me when I apply for research grants."

How might win-win thinking work in this incident? Wen Yan Rong's colleagues would have said, "It's great that he received the travel award! This means that Doug intends to follow through on his promise, since he indicated that there will be other awards. We should look at what Wen Yan Rong did to increase productivity to obtain ideas for our own sections. The fact that Wen Yan Rong got the award is a sign that things are going well in our organization." Doug probably thought that there would be this type of positive reaction when he introduced the incentive program. However, he met with a reaction common in China: "If something good happens to someone else, there is less likelihood of something good happening to me."

3. This is not a good answer. The Chinese managers are capable of applying statistics to quality control procedures and have no more difficulty learning such procedures than do people from any other country. Please choose again.

4. This statement is true and can be used as a starting point in one's thinking. However, it is too broad to be of much specific use in analyzing this incident. Some programs aimed at increasing productivity designed in one country will work in others, and some will not. The important task is to identify why some programs will work and why others will not and whether aspects of culture are involved. One of the alternatives deals with a possible difference between many people socialized in China compared with people socialized in the United States. Please choose again.

22 Whose Ideas Are These?

1. There is no indication in the incident that there is special difficulty in Chinese syntax regarding the type of relationship between one's ideas and ownership of those ideas. Indeed, no such syntactic form exists. Please choose again.

2. This is not the best answer. It may seem, in the short term, that the Chinese are inattentive about giving anything back in return for using someone's ideas. It is quite possible, however, that if John were patient, he would find that he would receive many benefits from Mr. Fang and other members of his collective. If, after he cools down, John reacts to Mr. Fang's behavior at the meeting in a gracious way, he will show that he understands how to make contributions to a collective. While a willingness to make a contribution to a collective may interfere with the praise that one's ego expects, there are more important concepts than "personal ego" in Chinese culture. Please choose again.

3. This is not a good answer. While Fang Da-chun was clearly using John's ideas at the meeting, this behavior did not stem

from Mr. Fang's expectations that he be compensated for looking after John. Mr. Fang's behavior stemmed from other aspects of Chinese culture. Please choose again.

4.   This is a good answer, but members of the validation sample felt that it would be difficult to integrate this into John's thinking as he considered drafting a letter. John might have been able to entertain this possibility after (a) calming down and (b) becoming more familiar with the expectations and obligations of membership in a collective. If John comes to be treated as a valued member of a collective in China, Mr. Fang may later show his appreciation for John's contributions. For example, Mr. Fang might introduce John to other Chinese businesspeople or to government officials who could be helpful to the American company for which John works, people John might not have access to without Mr. Fang's connections. It must constantly be kept in mind that behavior in China is based on membership in collectives. If John makes a contribution to the collective (e.g., his ideas), then he will eventually receive benefits that stem from his contributions. Mr. Fang did not feel the necessity to mention John's name when discussing his ideas since the ideas are now part of the knowledge held by the collective.

Mr. Fang, as a senior and high-status member of the collective, felt that he had the right—and obligation—to put forth the ideas of the collective in the most effective way possible at the meeting. Given the respect for age and status in China, it was much more effective for all concerned to have Mr. Fang present the ideas than for a much younger and less experienced person, particularly a foreigner, to present them. Mentioning the originator of the ideas might have been helpful to John's ego, but enhancing one individual's ego is not a priority in Chinese culture. Incidentally, this distinction between "source of good ideas" and "announcer of these in a public forum" is not unknown in the United States. A middle-level foreign service officer in the Department of State develops an important diplomatic initiative. Who announces this to the press and eventually to the general public, the midlevel officer or the secretary of state? If it is the latter, the officer knows that rewards will come at a later date and in a form different from immediate public recognition. In addition to this answer, there is another that helps with the interpretation of the incident. Please search the alternatives for this other helpful perspective.

5. This is a good explanation because it summarizes accurately the probable interpretations made by both John and Mr. Fang. Socialized in an individualistic culture, John has come to expect that his name will be associated with his contributions (Fiske, Kitayama, Markus, and Nisbett 1998). Socialized in a collectivist culture, Mr. Fang feels that once a person makes a contribution to a collective, the collective is considered the owner of the idea. Mr. Fang is aware that if John makes contributions, there will be various benefits that John will receive. These benefits might include introductions to high-status people, the seemingly sudden removal of "red tape" restrictions that were hampering John's plans, and information about investment opportunities that other Americans, who are not members of a Chinese collective, would never hear about.

    John feels that Mr. Fang has "stolen" his ideas. Such an idea would never occur to Mr. Fang, who felt that he was doing exactly the right thing to propose the ideas to the company. To the Chinese, "ideas" and "knowledge" are very abstract concepts. Neither ideas nor knowledge is treated as property with commercial value (Brislin 2000). When John shared his ideas with Mr. Fang, they became common knowledge, and there was no longer any explicit link between the idea and its originator.

    This incident and set of explanations help shed light on a problem that is puzzling to many teachers in the United States (and, more generally, North America and Europe). Teachers assign term papers and students hand them in without citing the sources of ideas presented in the paper. Given their perspective, teachers often write "plagiarism" on the papers, and the students can face disciplinary hearings. If the teachers were socialized in a collective culture, however, they would have a different perspective. Once knowledge is written down in books, it is available to all; there is not a great value placed on linking individual contributions with the names of the people who made the contributions. Making these links does not seem to be the best use of time to many collectivists.

The administrators of programs that sponsor students from collectivist cultures need to be aware of the problems that such students face. Students need to know the expectations for the preparation of term papers and the Western concept of plagiarism prior to the start of their formal studies (Althen 1995).

Part Six

The Workplace: Negotiations

23 Finding an Interested Buyer

George Gorski was excited to be in the People's Republic of China. This was his first visit, and he was interested in learning more about the culture and in making several contacts at the trade show. The opportunity to do business in China seemed like a real possibility. George had been very successful in his business dealings in the United States. He prided himself on the ability to "get things moving."

His first day at the trade show in Beijing had gone well. He was able to look around at the various displays of sporting equipment and get some idea of who he might approach. He was sure his products, tennis racquets with an unusual new design, would raise some eyebrows. On the second day he approached the company that he felt would be most responsive to his products and introduced himself to the general manager, a Mr. Li. Since he had read that the Chinese find getting down to business immediately too abrupt and rude, he began a casual conversation, eventually leading up to the topic of his products and suggesting how Mr. Li's company might benefit from using them. George then suggested that he arrange to get together with Mr. Li and provide more specifics and documentation on his products.

Mr. Li responded in fairly good English, "That would be interesting."

George felt a tremor of excitement as his mind reviewed the possibilities. Knowing that he had only a few days left in Beijing, George wanted to nail down a time. "When can we meet?" asked George.

"Ahh. This week is very busy," replied Mr. Li.

"It sure is," said George. "How about tomorrow morning?"

"Tomorrow?" queried Mr. Li. "If I have time, it would be good."

"It will only take about half an hour. How about ten o'clock? Meet you here."

"Tomorrow at ten o'clock?" asked Mr. Li, thoughtfully.

"Right," George said, "I'll see you then?"

"Hmm, yes; why don't you come by tomorrow."

"Okay," George responded, "It was nice meeting you."

George was anxious to see what would happen with Mr. Li. As ten o'clock rolled around, he approached Mr. Li's company's exhibit only to find that Mr. Li had some important business and was not able to meet with him. George called later that day and was told that Mr. Li was not available. Frustrated, George returned to his room for the evening.

What culturally based explanation might there be for this incident?

1. Mr. Li had very important business matters to attend to and was therefore unable to meet with George.

2. Relative to Hong Kong and Singapore, many businesspeople in the PRC are not very dependable about keeping their appointments.

3. Mr. Li was probably not interested in the products that George was introducing.

4. George failed to identify the one element in Mr. Li's behavior that showed interest.

5. George would have had a greater chance of success had he first developed a stronger relationship of trust.

Explanations for Finding an Interested Buyer begin on page 159.

24   Too Much Red Tape

Eric Dempski had recently established his first shop in China, in Guangzhou, and was optimistic about the prospects for his business, which would be making American-style cookies. He had been successful with several stores in Hong Kong and felt that his operations would prosper in a Chinese market, where economic reform was booming.

Although he had heard much about the red tape involved in doing business in China, he felt he could handle it. Indeed, he had relatively little difficulty in establishing his first shop after several weeks of completing paperwork, and he was open for business sooner than he had thought possible. The local bureaucrats with whom he dealt had seemed favorably impressed when he had indicated his desire to use local workers and even train local managers. His business was quite successful his first few months; people were eager to try Eric's unique product. Soon, a Tianbing Western Cookies shop owned by local businessmen opened, providing products and service similar to Eric's cookie shop and, hence, competition. It was time to expand the business. Eric felt there was enough demand for his cookies to open another shop in the city and wanted to get a jump on his new competition.

In order to expand the business, Eric needed to apply for additional building permits and so forth. He also needed to arrange for additional suppliers of the various ingredients used to make his cookies. To his dismay, however, Eric found that as he began applying for the necessary permits with the local government agencies, he was met with responses such as "We've never encountered this request" or "This procedure requires additional information." After several rounds of trying to obtain the permits, Eric became increasingly frustrated. After all, he had been successful in acquiring the permits to open his first shop. Moreover, his attempts to secure additional supply channels were as yet unfruitful. It seemed that all suppliers were "already at full capacity" or "unsure of future resources." What really amazed Eric was that Tianbing Cookies was announcing the opening of several shops around town. Eric thought that was particularly odd, considering that the owners of Tianbing Cookies had worked through the same government agency that he had.

What Chinese cultural concept will help Eric understand the cause of his frustration?

1. Eric did not work hard enough to compete with the local businessmen. In China hard work is very important, and Eric would have had to work vigorously to compete.

2. In China there is a cultural bias against foreigners and their products, especially foods. Because he is a foreigner, Eric's business suffered.

3. Eric had not cultivated the proper connections to survive the bureaucratic maze and succeed in business dealings.

4. It is not necessarily unethical for Chinese officials to accept bribes. Eric needed only to offer the right incentives to the authorities.

5. Because of the Chinese concept of harmony, it was a breach of etiquette for Eric to apply for expansion without first negotiating with the competition.

Explanations for Too Much Red Tape begin on page 160.

25   Request for a Price Concession

As she flew into Beijing, Patricia Worth was thinking of how she first became interested in doing business in China. Patricia was a member of a loosely knit group of people who liked to buy and fix up large, old houses. People in the group would help each other. For example, a person skilled in carpentry would assist someone else in exchange for help with the installation of air-conditioning. Patricia's contributions to this informal group centered on her skills with plumbing repairs. Patricia knew how to solve all but the most complex plumbing problems as long as she could find parts in her local hardware stores. Recently, the plumbing in her old house in Evanston, Illinois, had given her problems, and she had had terrible difficulty finding replacement parts for her kitchen plumbing. When she finally found some high-quality and reasonably priced parts with a "Made in China" stamp on them, she said to herself, Maybe there is a message here.

With the help of the Small Business Administration in nearby Chicago, Patricia began negotiations with manufacturing companies in Beijing. "People complain about the American government, but it has certainly helped me with my business plans," she told a friend. Her goal was to manufacture and market plumbing and electrical fixtures that would be especially suitable to those Americans buying and fixing up old homes. Her main contact person in Beijing was Lei Yingjin, an employee of one of the companies with which she was considering doing business. Mr. Lei had considerable English-language skill and was often asked by his company to be the liaison person when Americans, Australians, Canadians, and the British began correspondence related to business matters.

Shortly after Patricia's arrival, Mr. Lei helped her find an apartment. Later, he also introduced her to various government officials whose approval would eventually be necessary if business agreements were to be finalized. Mr. Lei also made arrangements for a dinner to which twelve people were invited, all of whom would be involved in the negotiations within his company.

During the first meeting at which actual business negotiations began, Patricia simply outlined the basics of her proposal. At the second meeting, when Patricia presented her opinions about reasonable unit prices for various plumbing fixtures, Mr. Lei began acting as the spokesperson for his company. He presented a counteroffer requesting a number of price concessions, some of which Patricia thought were unreasonable. She could recover her own costs and make a small profit, given Mr. Lei's suggestions, but she certainly would never join the group whose members were known to "do well in China." Patricia was aware that the Chinese are good businesspeople and hard bargainers, but she suspected that there was something going on in these negotiations that was unfamiliar to her. If Patricia asked you for your help in interpreting Mr. Lei's counteroffer and deciding how to respond, which of the following are reasonable replies you could make?

1.   Patricia recognizes the favors Mr. Lei has done for her, but her culture does not include the guidance that such favors should be returned.

2.   Mr. Lei feels that given the many favors he has done for Patricia, she should consider the possibility of returning the favors through the price concessions he requests.

3.   Patricia is familiar with the concept of returning favors, but she may not know the magnitude of the favors that Mr. Lei has arranged for her.

4.   Patricia's cultural background gives guidance regarding the practice of carefully returning each favor within a very short period from the time the favor was given.

5.   Mr. Lei's cultural background guides him in thinking that returning favors is not important.

Explanations for Request for a Price Concession begin on page 162.

26 Request for a Price Concession: The Sequel

I guess I survived that mistake, Patricia Worth said to herself after the meeting at which Lei Yingjin requested a major price concession (described in the previous incident). One reason Patricia was able to keep the negotiations going is that she had a very definite idea of her "bottom line." She had done extensive research on costs, markets, potential sales, and profits and had prepared clear tables and graphs that summarized this research. She was also able to present this information lucidly to the Chinese delegation and to show its members that no one would make money if Lei Yingjin's proposed figures were accepted.

Thus, Patricia became involved in a series of extended negotiation sessions. Over the months, she found herself becoming increasingly frustrated with the length of time taken up with the negotiations and her mounting expenses. Although she knew that the Chinese company was negotiating with other businesspeople who had related manufacturing plans, she was confident that she had a good plan and that the Chinese would eventually accept it.

At times, the negotiations seemed to go nowhere. Again and again, the Chinese chose to deal with generalities, such as "the best parts at reasonable prices, followed by effective marketing." There seemed to be an unwillingness, however, to discuss any details concerning what was meant by *best*, *reasonable*, and *effective*.

Then, unexpectedly, a member of the Chinese delegation challenged Patricia on the specifications of some showerheads that were part of her proposal for replacement plumbing parts. The delegate said, "The size of the threads in your proposal is such that they will initially fit well in older shower stalls, but over the long run there will be leakage and breakage. Our company will get a bad reputation." Patricia recognized that she had made a very small miscalculation concerning the size of the threads, but she also thought that this was a trivial matter that was easily corrected and was at any rate best left to the engineers who would eventually supervise production. Nevertheless, the members of the Chinese delegation spent hours on this point.

Patricia is experiencing a number of negotiation tactics that businesspeople from North America and Europe frequently encounter in China. What are these tactics?

1. The use of superordinate goals, challenging negotiator patience, and preference for discussing generalities rather than specific goals.

2. Win-win thinking, use of shame, and challenging negotiator patience.

3. Challenging negotiator patience, preference for generalities, and use of shame.

4. Use of superordinate goals, win-win thinking, and preference for generalities.

Explanations for Request for a Price Concession: The Sequel begin on page 163.

27 The Tea Party

David Evenson, manager of a supermarket chain based in Milwaukee, was eager to establish trade ties with the People's Republic of China, one of the fastest growing economies in the world. Through a Chinese employee, Wu Xin, David reached an agreement to import 2,400 two-ounce packages of Chinese green tea from Xin Cheng, an agricultural and animal products importing and exporting corporation in China's Zhejiang Province.

The shipment came in just in time for the Thanksgiving Day sales peak. David, a tea lover himself, was impressed by the quality of the tea, and the packaging was better than he had expected. He anticipated good sales of the tea in his stores. He even took the trouble to have Wu Xin write some bilingual ads for the tea, which ran in major local papers and on radio stations. However, because of the small size of the transaction, the transportation cost per unit was quite high. In order to profit from this transaction, David's accounting department suggested that the Chinese green tea be priced a little higher than the domestic and imported brands of tea they already sold. Mr. Sheng Jiao-ru, a representative from Xin Cheng, disagreed, suggesting that David cut the price to match other brands first; once the Chinese brand was established and recognized by the consumers, both sides could profit from economy of scale, selling a larger amount of tea at a lower cost per unit. David, who was unwilling to start out selling at a loss, decided to go with his accounting department's price proposal.

Three weeks later Sheng called David from China and learned that the green tea had not sold well at all and had been returned to the warehouse. Sheng again suggested that David try lowering the price, but David seemed to have lost interest in the project. Over the next several months, Sheng was unable to interest David in further deals, and he finally decided to let things rest for a time.

What cultural behavior explains David and Sheng Jiao-ru's failure to work out an arrangement that was satisfactorily profitable for both?

1. For the Chinese, in the development of a long-term market, a short-term loss does not matter very much. Sheng Jiao-ru assumed that David was just as willing as he was to take a short-term loss while looking for a product line and a market that would produce substantial long-term profits.

2. David quite reasonably felt that it was time to cut his losses and find something that would yield a quick profit. David felt that

he had already gone to a great deal of trouble to launch this product. It wasn't selling, so he didn't want to waste any more money or energy on it.

3. Sheng didn't understand how fickle the American market is. Americans' tastes change very rapidly. If a product doesn't catch on today, it's unlikely to become popular a month or a year from now, so there is no point in further attempts to try to convince people to buy the tea.

4. Chinese traders have limited opportunities to set up personal foreign contacts. Sheng was less likely than David to give up trying to make the tea sell, since promotions, or even his future employment, may depend on his establishing a strong business contact with David. While this was just a small venture to David, Sheng's future in his company was likely to be strongly affected by the success or failure of this deal.

5. David was annoyed with Sheng and his company, since David had to do all of the marketing work and had taken a loss. Sheng's company, on the other hand, had only to send the tea, collect the money, and do nothing.

Explanations for The Tea Party begin on page 165.

28   Connections in China

Over the past few months Aaron Roth had discovered that China was a very interesting place. He had made several visits to China to investigate the possibility of establishing a joint venture with a local partner, Mr. Lan. Aaron worked for a consumer electronics firm that was desirous of tapping the potential of the rising Chinese market.

During his most recent visit to China, Aaron's host, Mr. Lan, had again been very gracious, but Aaron was getting anxious to get to a clear discussion on various parameters of the possible joint venture. The first couple of days had been spent largely on sight-seeing excursions and banquets, where they had talked generally about possibilities—a tendency apparent in the several visits Aaron had made in the past months. Aaron knew that developing relationships with the Chinese took time, but he was beginning to wonder just how much time.

On the third day, they discussed more of the details and developed some alternatives that each would consider. During their visits, Aaron talked about some of the influential people in government and business that he knew. Mr. Lan hinted that perhaps it would be nice to visit Aaron's main plant in the United States, or to be introduced to some of Aaron's contacts in the United States. Aaron felt he had established a good relationship with Mr. Lan and wanted to invite him to the United States if the firm Aaron worked for decided to go ahead with the joint venture. Aaron left China with a fairly good understanding of what the options were and what Mr. Lan wanted. Mr. Lan had also given him a rather nice gift. He would weigh the factors of their discussion against other possibilities in China.

Eventually, Aaron's company decided against the joint venture in favor of other alternatives, and Aaron thanked Mr. Lan for his efforts. Several months later, he received a letter from Mr. Lan requesting a tour of Aaron's facilities and a letter of introduction to an influential senator that Aaron had mentioned to Mr. Lan on his last visit. Aaron felt that Mr. Lan's requests were rather odd. What might explain this situation?

1. Mr. Lan was being persistent about creating a joint venture. Persistence in negotiation is a common business practice in China.

2. Mr. Lan was angry that Aaron's firm had decided against the joint venture, and since he had been such a good host, Mr. Lan expected Aaron to reciprocate by hosting a trip for him to America.

3. Mr. Lan was simply interested in technology and wanted to gain all he could from Aaron's firm's operations and expertise.

4. Mr. Lan did not understand the nature of Aaron's relationship with the senator and was unaware that his request put Aaron in a difficult situation.

5. In his thinking, Mr. Lan had developed a personal relationship by hosting Aaron on several occasions and by providing a gift. Mr. Lan was simply calling on Aaron as an "old friend."

Explanations for Connections in China begin on page 168.

29   Are Ethical Issues Involved?

(This incident presupposes previous coverage of Fair Price? incident 16.)

Jack Williams and Herb Edwards had come to Shanghai to discuss a joint venture with a large Chinese electronics firm. Jack and Herb had been struck by the number of Americans who owned digital modems, and they thought to themselves that they could compete in the American market, given low labor costs in China. They also had in the back of their minds that digital modems might be attractive to consumers in China.

During their numerous meetings with executives and engineers of the electronics firm, Jack and Herb conscientiously gave presentations on their ideas. At about the seventh meeting, Herb began to notice that there were different engineers at every meeting. At about this same time, Jack noticed that the questions from the Chinese engineers were becoming more and more technical, and that he and Herb were finding it difficult to answer the questions without giving away trade secrets. After the twelfth meeting, Jack and Herb went out for a drink. Herb said, "I realize that the books about doing business in China say that the Chinese schedule meetings to gain specialized information about technology, but this is getting ridiculous. Don't they have any ethical code? How do they sleep at night?"

If you were asked to help Herb deal with his frustration, what might you say to him?

1. The engineers who began attending later meetings needed to catch up on the basics of the technology with their colleagues who had attended since the first meeting.

2. Herb is incorrect; the Chinese are looking for something else besides specialized information on the technology surrounding the manufacture of digital modems.

3. The Chinese are setting aside any guilt they are experiencing in their quest for advanced technological information.

4. The Chinese do not view their behavior as unethical, and they might point out that there are aspects of Jack's and Herb's behavior that could be looked upon as ethically troublesome.

5. The Chinese are trying to continue negotiations with Herb and Jack as they weigh the Americans' proposal against those of other companies interested in doing business in China.

Explanations for Are Ethical Issues Involved? begin on page 169.

Explanations for the Incidents in Part Six

23   Finding an Interested Buyer

1. This could be an explanation for what happened. However, there is not enough information provided to support this choice. Had he truly been interested and then unexpectedly detained by important business matters, it is most likely that Mr. Li would have left additional instructions suggesting a new time to meet or a method of contact. There is a much more likely alternative.

2. This is an inaccurate generalization. Although time concepts vary across national borders, businesspeople in China are generally just as dependable as are those in the United States. Dependability is considered a virtue in Chinese society. If Mr. Li believed that he had set a firm appointment with George, he would have been at the appointed place, and he would have been on time.

3. This is the best answer. There are two important cultural aspects at work in this interaction. The first is the issue of directness. In many situations where Americans tend to prefer directness, the Chinese are usually more comfortable with indirectness and ambiguity. The second is the concept of "face." Having face means that one is in good standing with others vis-à-vis his or her obligation to peers, subordinates, and superiors and is maintaining harmony in society as a whole. It is important to preserve one's face and, as much as possible, the face of others (Earley 1997).

   A Chinese person would have recognized that Mr. Li was clearly not interested in George's products at all. He had indicated his lack of interest by saying that he was busy. However, George failed to pick up the signal. Instead of saying "I am not interested" directly, Mr. Li chose a more polite way, according to Chinese cultural norms, to convey this message to George. Mr. Li did not want to tell George "no" directly and cause George to lose face (because his products were rejected). By failing to set a definite time for a follow-up meeting and by only half-agreeing to the specifics that George was pressing on him, Mr. Li was saying, in no uncertain terms, that he was not interested in pursuing the matter. George didn't have the cultural sensitivity to interpret Mr. Li's response correctly.

4. This is not a good explanation. Mr. Li didn't show any element of interest in the incident. George was the one who showed a lot of enthusiasm.

5. This is a true statement. However, it doesn't apply to the situation described in the incident. This was a trade show, where companies could establish initial contacts and introduce new products. Therefore, George really had no chance to develop a trusting relationship with Mr. Li, who was obviously not impressed by George's initial approach.

24 Too Much Red Tape

1. This is not a very good explanation. Though hard work is, of course, important for success in China as elsewhere, working harder wouldn't have helped Eric with his problem much at all. There is a better explanation.

2. This statement is simply not true. With growing purchasing power, people tend to buy more foreign-made products, which are generally believed to be of better quality. Actually, many Chinese people brag about the foreign products they own or use. Foreign products have become indicators of wealth or of a fashionable cosmopolitan lifestyle. When China's first Western fast-food restaurant, Kentucky Fried Chicken, opened in 1987, people waited forty-five minutes or more to order food. Western food is very trendy in China, and consuming it is considered a sign of increasing socioeconomic status, as more and more Chinese move into the middle class. Therefore, it is not true that there is a cultural bias against foreigners and their products.

3. This is the best answer. Connections are a very important instrument in doing business in China successfully. Without proper connections, you may never be able to get things done. If you don't know which government officials to contact, it might take you years and years to get all the stamps you need to start a new business. If you don't have proper connections, you may never be able to get electricity or other utilities for your new business. This is the problem Eric had in the incident. Appar-

ently, when Eric applied the first time, there was no local competition, and the relevant bureaucrats felt there was nothing to gain by withholding permits and licenses from him. When another person, with better *guanxi* (connections), came on the scene, however, they had much to gain by giving the advantage to the person with the guanxi (Tsang 1998).

Why are guanxi so important in China? First, they reflect the collectivist nature of Chinese society. People cultivate connections within and among groups to obtain a sense of belonging. Second, guanxi also give people a sense of security. In the absence of a legal system that promotes everyone's interests equally, security comes from a sense of trust and a long history among those who do business with one another (Luo and Chen 1996).

To succeed in business, or anything else in China, you must invest considerable amounts of time and effort cultivating guanxi with the appropriate officials. Sometimes you can have guanxi with a lot of people but not with a major decision maker, and consequently, nothing gets done. Different situations and circumstances dictate making effective use of different branches of one's guanxi network. In this case, Eric didn't have the necessary connections with the government officials and the local suppliers. Tianbing Cookies had no other competitive advantage except for good connections.

4. This is not the best answer, though there is some truth to it. Corruption has been of great concern to the Chinese for years. Anger about the corruption of public officials was one of the main rallying points during the 1989 demonstrations in TianAnMen Square.

    There is quite an extensive vocabulary to describe the various aspects of corruption; examples are *la guanxi* (draw connections) and *zou hou men* (go in through the back door). The Chinese government has attempted to curb bribery of officials with a number of different measures but with only limited success.

    Bribery has become so prevalent that it is now perhaps the biggest barrier to efficient allocation of economic resources and to further economic development. However, the Chinese never consider it ethical to accept bribes. Such corrupt practices exist because of ineffective law enforcement and numerous historical reasons. Our validation sample supported this alternative, perhaps because bribery is so widespread and is practiced by so many government officials that it appears to outsiders to be more acceptable than it is. Even people within a culture do not necessarily feel that all practices within their culture are ethical. It is probably true that Eric could have solved his problems with some well-placed bribes, but he would have created other, potentially more serious problems. Offering a bribe to the wrong official or at the wrong time could have serious negative consequences.

5. This is stretching the concept of group harmony much further than it can realistically go. With the introduction of a market economy, concepts such as competition are widely accepted in Chinese society. There might be different rules for competition, since the competitors will play the "game" by the rules of their own culture, but competition itself is certainly acceptable.

25 Request for a Price Concession

1. Patricia's culture gives her the guidance that returning favors is important, and so this is not a good answer. Returning favors is probably a cultural universal, and any cultural differences that may arise center on more specific issues such as when favors are returned or what is considered a large favor.

2. This is a good answer. Mr. Lei has provided Patricia with a considerable number of important favors. In his mind, Patricia now has a debt to him, a "guanxi debt." In his mind it is reasonable to ask Patricia to repay this debt in the form of the price concessions. In China, only a person who "has no face" would refuse to repay such favors when called upon to do so. It is possible that Mr. Lei, as part of good Chinese business practice, quite consciously arranged these favors in the hopes that Patricia would become obligated. Shenkar and Ronen (1993) advise that "Americans negotiating with the Chinese should avoid any 'orchestrated' accumulation of seemingly minor debts, and should instead repay perceived debts immediately" (200).

    The belief that in general favors should be returned is part of American culture, but the additional belief that favors should be returned immediately is not a high priority. For example, in her work with the informal group of Americans described in the first paragraph of the incident, Patricia might receive help from someone skilled in electrical wiring. It might be several years, however, before she would have the opportunity to pay back this favor through her expertise in plumbing, given that the electrician might not have a need until that time. There is also another good answer.

3. This is a good answer. Mr. Lei arranged some large favors for Patricia, but she might not recognize their magnitude and importance. For example, Patricia might take for granted that people can talk with government officials—"That's what they are there for!" This is the direction of her thinking according to her cultural background (recall the help she received from the Small Business Administration). Yet in China, talks with government officials are not so easily scheduled and carried out. China has been described as a land of walls and doors, and help with moving people through doors and around walls constitutes favors that must be returned (Fang 1999). The twelve-person dinner is also a large favor, signaling serious intent to negotiate, and Patricia might not recognize this. There is another good answer that helps with the interpretation of this incident.

4. Although Patricia should be familiar with the concept of returning favors, the additional directive that favors should be returned within a very short time period is not a high priority in terms of her cultural background. In American culture, it is acceptable to return favors at a later time, when circumstances suggest that a certain time is right. For example, in Patricia's informal group of people who repair old houses, she might receive help with electrical wiring during a certain year from a friend. She might not have the opportunity to return this favor with her expertise in plumbing until the friend needs help, and this may occur two or three years later. Please choose again.

5. Returning favors is very important in China, so this is not a good answer. Please choose again.

26   Request for a Price Concession: The Sequel

1. This is a good answer. Superordinate goals refer to clear outcomes that both parties in the negotiation want. At the same time, both parties realize that the efforts of people from all

sides are needed if the goals are to be attained. Superordinate goals also need to be clear to people so that everyone who is working toward the goals knows if progress is being made. Goals such as "manufacturing the best parts" or "effective marketing," if all parties are clearly committed to them and if they share ideas about specific steps toward their implementation, can have the status of superordinate goals.

There are also two tactics described in this incident that businesspeople from Europe and North America have observed while negotiating in China (Pye 1982; 1992). While it is always risky to make generalizations about people, since they may serve as dangerous stereotypes, it is reasonable to suggest that Chinese negotiators are more patient than their European and American counterparts. Let's take the more specific case of American negotiators. The Chinese know that Americans want to sign agreements as quickly as possible. Consequently, the Chinese will delay, playing on the Americans' impatience to "get things done."

The second tactic of the Chinese is their willingness to communicate at a very general level in the early stages of negotiations (Fang 1999). In China these early negotiations will often be carried out by very high-level people, who will ideally expect negotiating counterparts at the same high level. The Chinese will prefer speaking in generalities such as "the importance of cooperation," "the best products at competitive prices," and "more jobs for more workers." Americans, again following their "Let's get things done" approach, will want to deal with more specific issues. Examples would be "the availability of manufacturing plants," "supplies of raw materials," and "statistical quality control procedures." The Chinese often prefer coming to general agreements, which are to be followed by negotiations on specific details. Assuming that the negotiations on more specific details have begun, the original preference for general negotiations becomes tactical when the Chinese claim that the spirit of the general agreements is not being followed when they want concessions on specific points. The general advice for American negotiators is to be patient with the Chinese preference for general talks in early stages but to avoid agreements on general points that can be turned against them later in the negotiations.

2. You are correct on the latter two of the tactics (shame is discussed in alternative 3, patience in 1), but it is hard to see the use of win-win thinking in this negotiation. Win-win thinking refers to efforts that allow all of the parties to feel that they have done well in the negotiations (Pruitt 1998). Ideally, this thinking leads all the parties to conclude that they are winners in this negotiation. Sometimes win-win thinking involves compromises, sometimes it involves bringing in other issues of interest to one or more of the parties, and sometimes it involves examining the long-term self-interests of the other parties so that ways of satisfying those interests can be found. One of the assumptions of win-win thinking is that people who are satisfied with the results of negotiation will follow through on agreements. They will put their time, resources, and energy into implementing the agreements rather than into breaking them through noncompliance, legal challenges, delays, and so forth. Good negotiators, then, make sure that the other parties are satisfied with negotiation outcomes and feel well treated. In this incident, it is hard to see win-win thinking given the fact that the Chinese delegation is negotiating with other businesspeople and is challenging Patricia on details such as thread size. Please choose again.

3. This is a good answer. In addition to the tactics of patience and preference for generalities (discussed under the explanation for alternative 1), the Chinese may use shame to their advantage. The Chinese may try to find mistakes in a proposal, thinking that their negotiating counterparts will feel shame and will try to make amends for the mistakes. Consequently, the Chinese will spend a great deal of time discussing the implications of a small mistake (e.g., thread size in this incident) that the Americans might find trivial.

4. It is hard to see the presence of win-win thinking in this example (win-win thinking is discussed in alternative 2). Readers may want to consult that explanation and then choose another alternative or alternatives.

27 The Tea Party

1. This is one of two good answers. Chinese businesspeople often appear to be willing to commit what seem to Americans unrea-

sonable resources to developing a new market (Y. Zhu 1999). This fundamental difference in business practices has caused a great deal of tension and distrust between the Chinese and Americans in business dealings over the past two decades. From the Chinese point of view, a business relationship is a type of friendship; trust must be established and a "lifetime" of mutual benefits and obligations pursued. To Americans, a business relationship is primarily an opportunity for profits. If there is no profit within a reasonable amount of time, it makes sense for the relationship to end. There is a noticeable cultural difference in what constitutes "a reasonable amount of time" in which to show a profit. Americans have far less patience with an initially unprofitable venture than do the Chinese. Unlike Sheng's company, David's probably has shareholders to answer to and needs to show profits every quarter. In a sense, he doesn't have the leisure to develop long-term markets that his Chinese counterpart has.

One of our Chinese authors gives some historical perspective. There is an old Chinese saying: "You can hook the big fish with a long string." Chinese businesspeople are more willing to commit financial and human resources to developing a new potential market because they believe that their long-term investment will eventually lead them to large profits. Also, Chinese businesspeople view their relationships with their partners as friendships. Another old saying says, "There can be no deal, but we should be friends." Among business partners, trust and long-term relationships often take priority over monetary benefits. At the same time, trust and long-term friendships are believed to promote financial success on both sides.

In Chinese history, there are many stories about how people should be patient and wait for the right opportunity. One famous story is about the king of Yue, Gou Jian, and the king of Wu, Fu Chai, who occupied Gou's country. Fu Chai made the king of Yue his slave and required that he do the same work as all other slaves, for example, feeding horses and cleaning stables. Fu Chai did everything he could to humiliate Gou Jian. While going through all these sufferings, the king of Yue hung a piece of *dan* (gall bladder), which is very bitter, in his room. He would lick the dan every night before he went to sleep to remind himself of the bitterness of having somebody else occupy his country. He waited until the right moment and was eventually able to kill Fu Chai and restore himself to power.

This is a widely cited story when Chinese people talk about patience. Although it is an old story, the Chinese have internalized its teaching and have extended it into different aspects of life, for example, in doing business, in the workplace, and even in politics. In this incident, Sheng was willing to take a short-term loss while waiting for a potential profit. This is consistent with the Chinese philosophy of waiting patiently for the golden moment.

2.   This is one of two good answers. Like most Americans, David was not interested in business dealings that did not show promise of immediate or at least reasonably prompt and substantial profits. He had invested quite a bit of energy in a relatively small enterprise, and since it had not met with success, he was ready to give it up. Sheng, on the other hand, saw this not so much as a single enterprise, but the beginning of a larger one, and he therefore felt that more time and energy were justified to make the tea sell.

3.   There is no evidence in the incident for this answer. Chinese consumer behavior in the 1980s and 1990s has been fickle indeed, and Sheng should have been accustomed to that. Furthermore, the whole point of marketing is to change consumer behavior and to invent new tastes and trends. At any rate, we have no reason to believe that Sheng did not understand the nature of American markets, since his suggestions on pricing indicated that he knew that Americans were not willing to pay a lot for Chinese tea at that time.

4.   It may be true that opportunities to set up personal foreign contacts are limited, but the failure of this one enterprise was unlikely to threaten Sheng's future. Even as it becomes more of a market economy, China is still a collectivistic society. Sheng would be allowed many misadventures more serious and costly than this one before his job would be in any danger. Further, as China's economy continues to open and grow, this answer will become even less acceptable, since there will be many investors from outside China courting the attention of individuals like Sheng.

5. This is an unlikely answer. While there are many cultural differences between Chinese and American businesspeople, some basic concepts are still held in common. In both cultures, unless otherwise specified, the retailer is responsible for the marketing of the product, and exports are bought and paid for. Since this is common practice, David would have no reason to be annoyed with Sheng on these points, though he might be annoyed with himself for agreeing to the original terms.

28   Connections in China

1. It may be true that persistence in negotiation is a common business practice in China (Pye 1982, 1992; Fang 1999), but it is not the right explanation for this incident. Since Aaron had already made the decision to turn down the joint venture, there was no reason for Mr. Lan to be persistent.

2. This is not a good choice. In the business world, it is routine that some business deals are successful while some are not. Mr. Lan wasn't angry at Aaron just because his firm had turned down the project, because there was nothing personal involved. In turn, Aaron had no obligation to reciprocate Mr. Lan's hospitality with a trip to the United States.

3. This is not a good answer. While Chinese businesspeople are often very anxious to learn more about new technologies and will go to some lengths to get the chance to do so, there is no evidence in the incident to lead us to the conclusion that Mr. Lan had any such intentions.

4. This is not the best answer, though it has some interesting possibilities. Aaron mentioned on his trip that he knew an influential senator. A Chinese person, making the same sort of statement, would be implying that he might have some connections, *guanxi*, with this official that could be useful to his potential partner, should they decide to collaborate. However, such a statement made by an American should be interpreted with caution. Americans are very good at "networking." A person they know might be somebody they met at a function once, or someone they talk to fairly regularly on the phone. In this case, it is difficult for us to judge how close the relationship is between Aaron and the senator.

5. This is the best choice. This incident is a good illustration of "drawing" on interpersonal connections (*la guanxi*). Mr. Lan had spent time and money hosting Aaron. Banquets, excursions, and gift giving are popular ways of establishing guanxi in China. If a guest attends banquets and accepts gifts, presumably guanxi have been established. And once guanxi have been established, the relationship is considered to be a long-term one (Luo and Chen 1996). The parties involved are expected to fulfill their obligations if called upon to do so. In this case, Mr. Lan was trying to utilize the guanxi he thought he had established with Aaron.

From Aaron's point of view, he had simply accepted some hospitality, fairly routine in the business world, to lubricate deals and establish a congenial atmosphere for doing business. When the joint venture didn't develop, the relationship was over for him, and there were no further obligations attached to the hospitality he had accepted.

29   Are Ethical Issues Involved?

1. This is probably not accurate, for cultural reasons. In China if one engineer in a company knows some technological material, he or she is expected to share it with others. This would reflect the cooperation possible in a well-run company within a collectivistic culture (Triandis 1995b). An engineer who keeps technological knowledge to himself or herself is known as an uncooperative fellow worker. The engineers at the seventh meeting, then, would have learned from others about the material presented at the first six meetings. Please choose again.

2. In selecting this alternative, you may be on the right track, because the Chinese might have another agenda in requesting so many meetings. However, they *are* interested in using the meetings to learn advanced technological material concerning digital modems. Please choose again.

3. It is incorrect to say that the Chinese are setting aside guilt for a very simple reason—they don't feel any guilt in scheduling so many meetings in order to be exposed to advanced technology. It may be helpful to ask the question, "What might people from other cultures think about Herb's and Jack's ethical standards?" Please choose again.

4. This is a good alternative. The Chinese want to learn advanced technology, and they do not see any ethical difficulties in scheduling numerous meetings and asking pointed questions meant to discover such knowledge with businesspeople who are proposing joint ventures (Fang 1999). They might say, "This is just good business practice—to learn from others with advanced technology." They might also point out, "We feel that our practice is good business just as people from the United States (and many other parts of the world) feel that it is good practice to do business in China because of low labor costs." (See Kelley and Luo 1999 for a discussion of low labor costs.) The Chinese might then ask how Herb and Jack can sleep at night, given the wages they propose to pay Chinese workers compared with the wages they would have to pay American workers. You may also want to search for a second correct alternative.

5. This is a strong possibility. The Chinese may be maintaining contact with Herb and Jack while also negotiating with other companies. Scheduling meetings with these two Americans allows the Chinese to continue interactions (and to keep the two in China) while negotiations with other companies proceed. In addition, the Chinese may well use technical information learned from Herb and Jack to negotiate more effectively with the other companies! Such practices are viewed negatively by Americans, and complaints such as "They are stringing us along" and "They are taking advantage of our willingness to discuss technology" will be heard from businesspeople from the United States and elsewhere. However, scheduling meetings to learn about technology and using the newly gained knowledge during negotiations with other companies are accepted business practices in China, and foreign firms considering joint ventures with the Chinese should know about these practices.

Part Seven

Academia: Understanding Relationships with Authority

30 The Best Way to Learn

Bonnie Carson had been teaching high school English in Illinois for seven years when she decided that she needed a change of pace. The offer of a teaching job at a teachers' college in southern China sounded like a wonderful adventure.

Indeed, the change of scene was exciting, she loved the food, and there was much to see and do. Both her colleagues and her students seemed a bit shy around her, but Bonnie was sure that, in time, they would all come to be friends.

In the classroom, however, Bonnie was very frustrated. When she asked a question, the class was silent. Only if she called on a particular student would she get an answer, often a very good one. She couldn't understand why the students wouldn't volunteer, when they obviously knew the answers. They were very quiet when she was speaking in front of the class and never asked questions or interrupted with comments or opinions. However, as soon as the class ended, they would cluster around her desk to ask their questions one by one and offer suggestions about the lesson, staying for as much as half an hour after class.

Most frustrating of all, when Bonnie asked students to look over a dialogue for the next day's class, they were likely to memorize it. When she asked them to act out a dialogue, they were unwilling to do so *unless* they had memorized it. She tried to explain that memorization was an inefficient way to learn a foreign language, but the students just smiled and went on doing it their way.

If you were a colleague of Bonnie's with a bit more experience with Chinese learners, how would you help her deal with her Chinese students?

1. Explain that Chinese teaching methods are simply outdated. Bonnie should keep trying to break the students of their habit of memorizing everything and listening so passively, and she should try to introduce more effective learning strategies.

2. Explain to Bonnie that memorization and listening passively to teachers' lectures have brought her students considerable academic success. Suggest that she try to change her teaching style to bring it more in line with the learning style that obviously works for her students.

3. Explain to Bonnie the role that memorization plays in learning to read Chinese and the respect that is implied by "passive listening" postures in the classroom. Suggest that she try to strike a balance between what they are used to and good at and what she believes is more effective.

4. Explain to Bonnie that she is confusing cultural differences with developmental differences. The real difference is between teaching high school and college, not between Americans and the Chinese. Bonnie needs to adapt her style to more mature students, who can't be expected to shout out in class and be so flexible and carefree about their learning.

Explanations for The Best Way to Learn begin on page 184.

31 Docked Pay

Sara Wilson had been teaching English at a well-known Chinese university for four years. She and her husband, Ray, who taught at a teacher training college nearby, were highly thought of in their departments.

Sara and Ray were very excited when a paper they had written was accepted at a prestigious international language teaching conference. They knew that their institutions did not have money to support foreign staff in attending conferences, but since it was in Vancouver, they arranged to attend the conference on their way back from a visit to Ray's family in North Dakota, which they had planned to make anyway during the spring break.

Since the conference was to be held the second week after the beginning of Sara's spring term and since they could not afford to travel to the United States, back to China, out to Vancouver, and again back to China, she arranged with her department to return late for the spring semester. In fact, over the past four years, they had often left a few days or a week early for term breaks or returned a few days late, so they were quite sure there would be no problems.

Sara arranged to have colleagues cover the classes she would be missing. In return, she promised to teach classes for them at a later date. She also arranged to have assignments given to her writing classes by the substitute teacher, even though that meant that piles of work would be waiting for her upon her return. She got permission from the Foreign Affairs Office at her school to return late. Ray made similar arrangements at his college, and they set off to enjoy their holidays.

The presentation went very well, and Sara and Ray were proud to represent their Chinese institutions, which they felt were excellent but which had never before sent speakers to this conference. Sara was astounded when she got her first pay packet after her return to school to discover that she had been docked two weeks' pay. When she complained, she was told that she had missed two weeks of work and so, of course, had not been paid for it. Sara argued that she had been on professional business, which had made the school look good, that she had made up every scrap of work and arranged to have all her classes taught, that she had essentially fulfilled her duties, and that she had received permission from her department and the Foreign Affairs Office in advance. She also expressed her annoyance that she was being treated as an hourly worker, not the professional she was. Sara was unable to convince the authorities that she had been mistreated and finally had to accept that she would not get her back pay.

What is a possible explanation, having to do with cultural differences in policy issues, for this incident?

1.　The Foreign Affairs Office was becoming increasingly annoyed with Sara's early departures and late arrivals each term. Since the authorities had never complained about their late arrivals and early departures before, Sara and Ray mistook the silence and leniency as license to continue. Returning to class two weeks late was pushing the authorities too far; they had to take some punitive action.

2.　As North Americans, Sara and Ray were more likely than their Chinese counterparts to feel that terms of a contract were to be taken more as vague, flexible guidelines than as hard-and-fast rules.

3.　The Chinese authorities felt that Sara and Ray's paper was written by their own decision, not as part of their professional duties. Thus, their attendance at the conference was personal, not professional, business.

4.　The Chinese authorities wanted to discourage foreign teachers from doing research and attending conferences because it took their energy away from teaching, which was their first responsibility.

5.　In China, everyone, professionals or manual laborers, is considered an hourly wage earner. A worker who is away from his or her machine for two days will be docked two days' pay. A teacher who is away from her or his classes for two weeks will be docked two weeks' pay.

Explanations for Docked Pay begin on page 186.

32   Moving Too Fast

Dr. Thomas Thurmon was a fifty-year-old full professor in the sociology department at a major American public university. He was a popular professor who had a reputation for working well with, and devoting time to, his students.

Meng Jiang-ping from Shanghai had been working with Dr. Thurmon for three years as one of his research assistants. One day, Jiang-ping knocked on Dr. Thurmon's door and introduced him to Qi Liwen, who had recently arrived from Shanghai. Jiang-ping mentioned that he and Liwen had been students together in China and had been in correspondence over the last three years.

Dr. Thurmon asked Liwen if his trip had been pleasant. He then asked about Liwen's research interests. When Liwen responded that he was interested in village politics in rural China, Dr. Thurmon suggested that he contact Dr. Harris in the political science department. "I'll call her, if you prefer, Liwen, or you could contact her directly. She is very approachable. She has an interest in politics in small communities, so she may be able to suggest some theoretical concepts that will be useful to you."

Liwen responded that it would be very nice if Dr. Thurmon put in a call indicating to Dr. Harris that a student from China would be stopping by during her office hours. After this phone call was made, Jiang-ping and Liwen left Dr. Thurmon's office.

About a week later, Liwen stopped by Dr. Thurmon's office. During his conversation with Dr. Thurmon, Liwen asked Dr. Thurmon if he would write a letter of recommendation for him that would support his application for a teaching assistantship in the sociology department. Dr. Thurmon felt uncomfortable responding to this request.

If Dr. Thurmon asked you if there was something cultural going on, how would you respond?

1. From Dr. Thurmon's point of view, Liwen was making a request that was inappropriate for the amount of time the two had known each other.

2. Chinese students from Shanghai are noticeably more direct and assertive than people from other parts of China.

3. Jiang-ping should have prepared Dr. Thurmon for this type of request from Liwen.

4.   From Liwen's point of view, Dr. Thurmon had indicated that he would be willing to follow through on requests for favors such as this letter of recommendation.

5.   Liwen was taking unfair advantage of his relationship with Jiang-ping.

Explanations for Moving Too Fast begin on page 188.

33   Thank You for Your Service

Since September Stephanie Nelson had been working at a fairly large university that was considered highly prestigious in the region. She was an experienced and qualified English as a foreign language (EFL) teacher in her midthirties who had taught English as a second language (ESL) in both the United States and Canada. She'd had enough experience working with Chinese students in those countries to be able to give very helpful, specific advice about Chinese learners' problems with English.

Everything she had heard about how hardworking and enthusiastic Chinese university students proved to be true, and word got back to her that her students had spoken highly of her classes when asked by the department and university authorities. Stephanie got along reasonably well with all of her colleagues and very well with some of them. She was writing a paper together with Zheng Xi, one of the younger teachers, about a class that they were team-teaching that semester. Steph's biggest project was a peer-observation and -training program for the young teachers. She had initiated the program and had gotten enthusiastic support from another American and two Chinese colleagues. Stephanie was compiling training materials, with lots of feedback from one of the Chinese. Although the program was going very well, Steph knew it would take another year before the materials would be finished, the Chinese mentors trained, and the program well enough under way to be self-perpetuating.

Although she complained sometimes to her non-Chinese colleagues about how unattractive the city was and about the dry and dusty winter, she was thoroughly glad that the university had accepted her application to come to China to teach English, and as early as October she had mentioned to the department head and other leaders that she would like to extend her contract for a second year.

In February some of her non-Chinese colleagues mentioned having been formally offered positions for the next year. One of them was on a Fulbright, two were sponsored by the German government, and another was on a two-year research and teaching exchange program between her college and the Chinese university, so Steph wasn't too surprised that their jobs should be formally decided before hers. She was, after all, a free agent and had only made a one-year commitment initially. She was confident that, given her strong qualifications and excellent performance, her contract would be extended for a second year.

In early March at a department meeting, she and her colleagues were given a rundown of the foreign teachers that had been hired for the coming fall. The list did not include Stephanie but did include a young woman named Darcie Conklin, who was about to graduate from a college none of them had ever heard of, with a degree in economics and political science. While Steph was still in shock from getting the news in this particular way, the department head thanked her for her excellent service and asked her what she planned to do after she finished in July, as if nothing were out of order.

Stephanie was angry, hurt, and bewildered. Why in the world would she be passed over for a completely inexperienced and unqualified replacement? It was some comfort to her that her foreign colleagues were enraged. They asked, first privately among their closer Chinese colleagues and later more publicly, why a qualified teacher was being let go and being replaced by an unqualified nonteacher. The answer they received was that Darcie was the daughter of a man whom one of the department leaders, Wu Tian, had met while in the United States as a visiting scholar. Evidently, Professor Wu's son was going to be sponsored to study at the same U.S. college Darcie was graduating from and was going to be living with the Conklins. While Lao Wu had been in the United States, Darcie, then seventeen, had said she would like to go to China some day. Lao Wu knew she was about to graduate and had offered her the teaching job in December. After discussing it at length with her parents and friends, Darcie had accepted the job in early March. Some of the younger Chinese faculty seemed mildly annoyed when told the story, but it turned out that they objected not to Steph's mistreatment but to the unfairness of Lao Wu's undistinguished and untalented son having the chance to study in an English-speaking country instead of one of them. None of them seemed to feel that Stephanie had been unfairly treated. After all, she had never been promised a job, and she didn't have any financial backing from a foreign institution to make it worthwhile for the university to keep her on.

As the details of the story came out, the foreign faculty were galvanized. They complained to the Foreign Affairs Office, to anyone who would listen in the department—even to one of the university vice presidents who came to a banquet they attended—that the department's treatment of Stephanie was unprofessional, underhanded, and overtly corrupt. They argued that scores of Chinese English majors at the university were being insulted and deprived of a decent education because of one corrupt official. They claimed that if Steph left, the promising peer-observation and -training program that she had initiated would inevitably end, which would be a tragedy for the entire department. While the Chinese faculty agreed about the loss of the program and sympathized with Steph, most were embarrassed by the intensity of the foreign teachers' objections and began to draw away. By the end of the spring term, the department was divided, Zheng Xi and Steph's paper had been abandoned, and the foreign teachers who were staying on for the next year were unenthusiastic and depressed at the prospect of spending another year in a place where personal interest and corruption were tolerated and professionalism was devalued.

What explanation might you offer to the foreign faculty at this school?

1.   The Chinese leaders found Steph's "innovations" meddlesome. They were anxious to get rid of her.

2.   The Chinese, more than Americans, feel that those with positions of power have the right to use those positions as they see fit, even if it seems illogical to subordinates.

3.   Obviously, the Chinese at the university where Steph was teaching, like many people, believed that anyone who could speak English could teach it, so it didn't make any difference who they hired.

4.   The authorities were concerned that Steph's relationship with Zheng Xi might have become too intimate. It is generally not advisable to coauthor a paper with only one Chinese colleague or to put yourself in a position where you are spending any amount of time behind closed doors with a single co-worker.

5.   The Chinese at this university were simply corrupt. They took corruption for granted and didn't value good work. Steph was lucky to get out. She—and her foreign colleagues—should look for more congenial positions at other Chinese universities.

Explanations for Thank You for Your Service begin on page 190.

34 Don't Do It, Xiao Zhang

Laura has been teaching English in a Chinese university for over a year. As an undergraduate, she majored in linguistics at her American university, studied Chinese for two years, and spent one semester of her junior year studying at a university in another Chinese city. She enjoys China and her teaching, and she feels that her reasonably good Chinese skills and her familiarity with the culture have made life comparatively easy for her. She gets along well with both her Chinese and Western colleagues and feels especially lucky that her department head, Liu Dehua, has had considerable experience working with Westerners in China, the United States, and England. She has heard that many other foreign teachers in China have cold or difficult relationships with their colleagues and bosses, but Liu Dehua seems at ease with her and the other Western teachers.

During Laura's second year of teaching, Professor Liu asks her to help Zhang Qian, one of Laura's Chinese colleagues, with a new course he is teaching. While working closely together on developing the course, they fall in love. Realizing that this situation will not be looked upon favorably by their co-workers or students, they keep the relationship secret. They continue to see each other but behave very discreetly. After several months, they decide that they would like to get married. Zhang Qian thinks that it would be wise to get some advice about how to proceed. He and Liu Dehua have a good relationship, and Laura likes and trusts Professor Liu as well. In addition, he is one of the first people they will have to notify officially to get permission and documents for their marriage, so Zhang Qian goes to see him.

When Zhang Qian returns he is reluctant to tell Laura what they talked about. He seems upset and tired, so Laura drops the subject, but the next day as Laura and Zhang Qian are leaving the classroom building together, Liu Dehua asks Zhang Qian to meet with him after lunch. Zhang Qian is gone for hours, and when Laura sees him later in the afternoon, he finally tells her that Liu Dehua is trying very hard to convince him to abandon his foolish idea of marrying a foreigner and has presented numerous reasons why the relationship will not work. He has gone so far as to offer to arrange an exciting transfer to Beijing for a year to give Zhang Qian some time to think about things. Laura is very upset, as she has believed that Liu Dehua likes and respects her. She doesn't understand why he would interfere in her personal life in this cruel way.

How would you explain Liu Dehua's behavior to Laura?

1. Liu Dehua has just pretended to like Laura because they have to work together. Laura doesn't understand enough about Chinese culture and behavior to tell the difference between true camaraderie and a cordial professional relationship.

2. Liu Dehua truly likes and respects Laura, which is why he doesn't want her to be used. Professor Liu suspects Zhang Qian of taking advantage of Laura's affection to get a passport and visa to the United States. His efforts to convince Zhang Qian to abandon her are an attempt to assess the depth of Zhang Qian's commitment.

3. Like many Chinese, even teachers of English who have been abroad and are familiar with Western ways, Liu Dehua is still deeply suspicious of foreigners. He doesn't want one of his teachers to marry one.

4. As Zhang Qian's boss, Liu Dehua feels it is his duty to behave in a fatherly way toward Xiao Zhang. To Professor Liu, this means warning him of all the potential difficulties involved in marrying a non-Chinese.

5. Liu Dehua truly believes the relationship will not last. He is trying to persuade Zhang Qian to break up with Laura before the relationship becomes public, so there will be less loss of face for everyone.

Explanations for Don't Do It, Xiao Zhang begin on page 193.

35 A Right to Be Angry?

Dr. Mary Bradford was a senior professor working as a permanent staff member at a research laboratory that was dependent on successful competition for grants from business and government sources. The organization that employed her had a large number of regulations, especially in the hiring of research assistants, but no more than similar organizations in other parts of the United States. One regulation was that newly hired employees be considered "on probation" for the first two years of employment. After this period, if the employees become permanent, they have first claim to information about promotions within the organization. If an employee has the necessary qualifications for a higher-level job, the organization's policy dictates that the employer (e.g., a senior professor) must indicate why an employee is not being hired, should that employee not be offered the job.

Dr. Bradford once secured a one-year grant for a study of the labor force in China. She needed two research assistants, but no one in the organization wanted the jobs since they were only for one year, so she successfully recruited two new people, "Stella" Chang, from Beijing, and Louise Lake, from New York City. At the time of their hiring, both were told that the jobs were for one year, and they were also told of the company policy (summarized in the first paragraph).

Stella and Louise worked hard, and Dr. Bradford mentioned to both that she would be pleased to write strong letters of recommendation for them in their future job searches. At the beginning of about the tenth month of the grant, Dr. Bradford secured another contract for a five-year study of Chinese textile imports and exports, and she also learned that the contract could be renewable beyond the first five years. Dr. Bradford again advertised for two research assistants. Stella and Louise both applied. However, a number of highly qualified employees who had passed the two-year probationary period also applied, attracted by the long-term possibilities of this new grant. Dr. Bradford chose two of these post-probation applicants and informed Stella and Louise of her decision. Although she said nothing, Stella displayed some anger in her face, and during the final two months of the grant was no longer a cooperative employee or co-worker. Louise continued working hard and remained on congenial terms with Dr. Bradford. When Dr. Bradford eventually wrote letters about Louise and Stella for their applications for other jobs, her letter for Louise was noticeably more positive.

Are there cultural factors that can be called upon to help explain the opposite reactions of Stella and Louise during the last two months of their employment with Dr. Bradford?

1. Given Stella's cultural background, anger was justified under these circumstances.

2. Given Louise's cultural background, keeping up positive relations with employers was wise behavior.

3. Given Dr. Bradford's cultural background, she was not careful enough to explain organizational policy to Stella and Louise.

4. Given Louise's cultural background, employment with one or with a very small number of organizations over the course of her working life is expected.

5. Given Stella's cultural background, Dr. Bradford's personal relationship with her should have been as important in hiring decisions as written organizational policy.

Explanations for A Right to Be Angry? begin on page 196.

Explanations for the Incidents in Part Seven

30   The Best Way to Learn

1. This is not the best answer. It's true that Chinese teaching methodology does not take into account much of what is "known" about learning, as based on research in Western settings. It's also true that many Chinese students rely on methods of learning that have been used for thousands of years. However, before deciding that these methods are old-fashioned, counterproductive, and best discarded, Bonnie ought to think about why they have been around so long and what she might learn from them. Bonnie should try to introduce what she considers to be more effective learning strategies, but she should also be sensitive to resistance to those strategies, and she should be ready to accept that what works in the West may not be so effective for her Chinese students.

2. This is not a bad answer. Chinese students' faith in memorization and passive listening and note taking is well founded, especially when they have been among the less than 1 percent of Chinese citizens who survived the examinations system and got into universities and colleges. Their learning styles have served them well, and they would need much persuasion to abandon them. However, it is unlikely that Bonnie, with her Western training and experiences, would be able to change suddenly to become a successful teacher in the Chinese style. What's more, the Chinese would probably be unhappy if she did. The reason that Westerners are invited to teach English in China is to introduce new ideas and methods of teaching. Bonnie's students and colleagues may have been dubious of and reluctant to adopt her classroom style, but they valued her presence nevertheless. Look for an alternative that doesn't require Bonnie to abandon her ideas of good teaching.

3. This is the best answer. Bonnie needs to understand that the Chinese language, with its thousands of unique characters, requires that any educated person have a prodigious memory. From the earliest days of their primary school education, Chinese students memorize not only the multiplication tables, as American students do, but the stroke-by-stroke pattern of every word in their language. The fact that the students had so

many questions and comments after the class attests to the fact that they were actively listening after all, even if they didn't appear to be. Traditionally in China the teacher has the knowledge, and it is his or her duty to transfer it to the students. For students to ask questions may imply that the teacher has not explained things clearly enough and has therefore failed in his or her duty. When students sit quietly and listen, they are simply showing respect (Tobin, Wu, and Davidson 1989). They do sometimes get bored and lost, of course, so they may welcome a teaching style that encourages more interaction with the teacher at some points in the lesson.

Bonnie should try to strike a balance between doing what she thinks is best for her students and honoring their culturally conditioned learning styles. Many teachers who deal with learners from other cultures find that they can get students to try new ways of doing things if they are explicit about the reasons for wanting the students to do so. It is especially effective if the teacher can say, "I know that your Chinese teachers generally do such and such, but I'd like to try it this way because...." Bonnie will need a cultural informant to help her understand how a Chinese teacher would typically handle certain types of teaching points, and she will also need to think about what teaching and learning behaviors she is most eager to change.

One of the Chinese authors' perspective is that with economic reforms and the disappearance of the job assignment system, students need to learn to be outgoing, aggressive, and competitive (Schoonhals 1994). To be competitive in the market, they need skills that cannot be acquired by simply memorizing textbooks and lectures (Hofstede and Bond 1988). Foreign lecturers are hired with the expectation that they can be the catalyst of a reform process in education. However, the process should be evolutionary instead of revolutionary. Bonnie should try to maintain a balance between what Chinese students are used to and her more interactive teaching method.

She could, for example, allow students to memorize dialogues and role plays but then insist that they do some improvisation from the memorized text. There is nothing wrong with memorization that is not mindless, and it would be a shame for Bonnie not to take advantage of her students' ability to memorize new vocabulary, songs, and texts.

4. This is not a good answer. The classroom behaviors exhibited by Bonnie's students are typical of Chinese learners of all ages and are frequently mentioned sources of frustration for teachers new to China. If anything, teachers feel that their Chinese college-age students behave more like American high school students than like American college students.

31   Docked Pay

1. This is one of two good answers. It is wise for foreign employees of Chinese universities to realize that while they are given much special treatment—privileges not afforded their Chinese colleagues and leniency in many situations where their Chinese colleagues might be reprimanded quite harshly—there is a limit. If the authorities had *not* responded to this very late return to the job, they might have lost face in front of the Chinese faculty with whom they also had to maintain a healthy relationship (Earley 1997). There is little doubt that Sara's Chinese colleagues resented what must have seemed to them as flaunting her special status. The Foreign Affairs Office must also have been concerned that other foreign teachers would see Sara and Ray "getting away with it" and want to extend their vacations, too.

2. On the contrary, as North Americans, Sara and Ray would be culturally conditioned to view contracts as binding, rather than as the more flexible expressions of intention that the Chinese often seem to see. Westerners in China are often confused by the lack of clearly stated rules and policies, the lack of a contract, or, more often in recent years, the flexibility of the contract that exists. It is often hard for them to understand when the Chinese take a rule seriously and when they are willing to bend it. It is also very difficult, at times, to tell when one's behavior is problematic and when it is not, especially since many of the rules that apply to the Chinese do not apply to foreigners in China and vice versa.

    Most likely Sara's and Ray's expectations about contracts had been upset several times in the past. This would lead to a sense that the contract meant little or nothing, and that as long as the work was taken care of, the details were unimportant. Sara would have been wise to consult with a Chinese colleague about whether the missed days at the beginning and end of term were upsetting to her colleagues or were a problem with the authorities. This would have avoided a public expression of annoyance (the withheld pay) on the part of the authorities.

3. This is one of two good answers. Although Sara and Ray attended the conference as the representatives of the school, they did so on their own authority, just as they wrote the paper on their own personal initiative. Their attendance at the conference was seen as a personal decision.

Authority is a very important concept in the hierarchical structure of Chinese society (Chinese Culture Connection 1987). Authorities at different levels do not expect to be ignored or overruled. Sara and Ray might have felt that they had been taking admirable initiative to work on their paper and make accommodations at work for the time they were away. However, in the eyes of the school authorities, they were exercising too much freedom without consent from their superiors. Their behavior was possibly considered as a challenge to those authorities.

Whereas Chinese faculty members are encouraged and supported in their efforts to present and publish research findings to enhance the reputation of their universities, foreign faculty are not seen as "belonging" to the university in the same way. In fact, it is very rare for a non-Chinese faculty member to stay at the same institution for more than two or three years, since the authorities disapprove of longer appointments. Therefore, any work they do besides what their institution requires of them is their own business. Sara and Ray understood that their schools could not help them financially to attend the conference, but they probably did not appreciate the extent of the disinterest in their attendance. Actually, the fact that Sara was attending a prestigious international conference rather than a relative's wedding or a rock concert was irrelevant in this case, and it simply served to confuse the issue. While the conference was the reason she was late, it was not the reason she was penalized. Look for another alternative that will suggest why she was penalized.

4. The Chinese don't support foreign teachers in doing research or attending international conferences, but neither do they dis-

courage it. In fact, foreign faculty at some institutions are strongly encouraged to attend conferences within China, to copresent with Chinese colleagues, and to become involved with ongoing research and materials design projects within their departments, in addition to teaching.

It would have been easy for Sara to assume that she was being penalized for attending a conference, when in fact the issue was accumulated absences in violation of the rules. It was simply bad timing that caused her to be penalized when she was at a conference. If the conference had been the only time in four years that she had been late returning from break, and if she had made all the arrangements that she did to cover her classes, she would probably not have been penalized.

5. This is not really a very good answer. The issue is more complex than this. While foreign teachers' contracts at universities do stipulate the number of hours they must teach, the contracts are notoriously flexible and one duty is often substituted for another with the agreement of employer and employee. This is also true, to some extent, for workers in what Americans would generally consider hourly wage jobs. This situation, however, is changing with rapid economic reforms.

32   Moving Too Fast

1. This is a good answer. From Dr. Thurmon's viewpoint, a student should ask for a letter of recommendation only after interacting with the professor for a period of time, so that the professor, as an individual, will have firsthand knowledge about the student. In the United States, letters of recommendation of this sort almost always ask, "How long have you known the applicant, and in what capacities?" Dr. Thurmon knew that if he answered "I have had two meetings with the student over a period of one week," then the recommendation would not be taken seriously by people reading it. In addition, Dr. Thurmon was likely to say to himself, What intelligent things can I say about a student with whom I have had only two meetings? Look for another good answer that explains Liwen's viewpoint.

2. While there are generalizations like this about people from different parts of China, they are rarely useful in shedding light on critical incidents of this sort. There are better answers that re-

spond more directly to the question, "Is there anything cultural going on?" Please choose again.

3. This is an interesting answer and one that can't be entirely dismissed. However, this type of preparation happens so infrequently that we can't assume that it will occur often enough to be a realistic expectation for people who interact frequently with individuals from different cultural backgrounds (Brislin and Yoshida 1994). Behaviors guided by culture are much like the air we breathe—we don't think about them very much and have had little practice articulating the exact reasons for difficulties when they occur. It would have been asking a great deal of Jiang-ping for him to (a) understand differences in his, Liwen's, and Dr. Thurmon's cultural orientation and (b) expect him to articulate cultural differences in such a way so that both Liwen and Dr. Thurmon could have been prepared for possible misunderstandings. Please choose again.

4. This is one of two good answers. From Liwen's viewpoint, Dr. Thurmon's behavior had indicated that membership was being offered in Thurmon's "inner circle" of students (Brislin 2000). Consequently, Liwen felt he could then engage in requests typical of such membership, like a request for a letter of recommendation. What were these behaviors? One would be Dr. Thurmon's expressing an interest in Liwen's research and asking questions about it. Another would be the offer to phone another professor, thereby establishing a connection with Dr. Harris. Perhaps another might be Dr. Thurmon's use of Liwen's first name. These behaviors emanating from a high-status figure in China are markers that a close superior-subordinate relationship is being offered.

    From Dr. Thurmon's viewpoint, he was simply being pleasant and sociable according to American norms. He has probably made polite inquiries about research interests and made telephone calls for hundreds of students, so his efforts on Liwen's behalf did not have any special meaning to him. These behaviors are far less common in initial interactions in China, so Liwen attributed Dr. Thurmon's kindnesses as having been "specially directed to me."

    There is another reason Liwen felt justified in going to Dr.

Thurmon for help even though he had only talked to him once. Since his good friend had been Dr. Thurmon's research assistant for three years, Liwen automatically included Dr. Thurmon in his *guanxi* (connections) network and considered him a person he could count on for help. He had no idea that Dr. Thurmon did not share those assumptions.

Incidentally, from Liwen's viewpoint, Dr. Thurmon had several options available for writing a letter based on such a short relationship. Dr. Thurmon might be expected to talk to Jiang-ping to find out key information that would be put into a letter of recommendation. In effect, the letter would come out of collective membership—(Thurmon, Liwen, and Jiang-ping)— not just the relationship between two individuals (Luo and Chen 1996). Another possibility, one that is often pursued in China, is that the applicant, in this case Liwen, would write the letter himself, and Dr. Thurmon would merely read it over and, if he found nothing objectionable, sign it. The fact is, the recommendation letter is a very new concept in China. Only students applying to an overseas school would even understand what it is. Recommendations or referrals in China are usually done in person. Liwen's uncle might, for example, recommend him for a job in the uncle's friend's company. In this case, the degree of closeness between Liwen's uncle and his friend would be essential. What his uncle said about him would not really be that important. Chinese usually assume that the same is true about recommendation letters. Who writes the letter is thought to be much more important than its content. When Liwen came to Dr. Thurmon, he hoped that Dr. Thurmon's personal influence would help him to get the assistantship. He may still not have realized that it was the content of the letter that counted.

5. This is not a good answer because people with relationships going back a number of years, such as former classmates, are expected to help each other in China. Of course, Liwen would eventually be expected to return the favors granted by Jiang-ping. Please choose again.

33   Thank You for Your Service

1. There is no evidence in the incident that Steph's innovative contributions were anything but welcome. It is true that the

university authorities sometimes do not agree with foreign language department faculty about what is best for the students, but that does not appear to be the case here. In fact, it is quite clear that the decision to release Stephanie was made within the department for reasons having to do with department personnel. Stephanie had proceeded wisely, by working closely together with Chinese colleagues. She was thus unlikely to push an idea that was controversial or unwelcome to more distant university authorities, since her colleagues could act as her cultural informants every step of the way.

2. This is the best answer. The Chinese are comparatively less likely to question the decisions of those in authority than are Americans (Bond 1986; Chinese Culture Connection 1987). This affords those in positions of responsibility more latitude in decisions than Americans might have. It is to be expected that, having paid his dues to reach such a position of authority, including accepting decisions from his own superiors that annoyed him, Wu Tian would take advantage of his position to secure opportunities for those in his collective.

    It is worth noting that Lao Wu's actions did not seem as illogical or inexplicable to the Chinese faculty as they did to the foreign staff. That colleagues they respected were unsurprised by Steph's treatment could have alerted the foreigners that they were encountering cultural differences. The Chinese faculty knew that ordinarily, Professor Wu Tian would have looked for opportunities to strengthen the English department, since he was a member of that collective. However, when what was best for a member of his family—the smaller, more immediate, and more important collective—conflicted with what was best for the larger collective composed of his colleagues, co-workers, and students, there was no question about what took precedence. Stephanie, being a foreigner, was not seen as being entitled to any sort of consideration as a member of the collective, since she was by definition an outsider. Lao Wu and the other English department personnel at his level may have been concerned about the annoyance of the Chinese faculty, but they sincerely did not care what the foreign teachers thought about their decision. Since Steph had no financial backing but was merely a free agent, there was no threat of retribution from her sponsoring agency, and Lao Wu's action would not be perceived by his Chinese colleagues as a real threat to the well-being of those in his work collective. Of course, a leader who too often uses his authority for personal or family gain at the expense of the work unit will lose the respect and cooperation of his subordinates and others at all levels of the hierarchy, making it harder for him to reach both personal and professional goals (Dorfman 1996).

3. This answer was fairly strongly supported by our validation sample. Certainly it is the impression of many Westerners that the Chinese hire anyone who "looks like an English speaker" and has a suitable passport. White Americans, British, and Australians are first choices. Very obviously more qualified Chinese Americans may be passed over as "nonnative speakers," even if they know only English and not a word of Chinese. On the other hand, more and more Chinese universities are insisting that applicants hold an M.A. or even a Ph.D., though they don't necessarily care if the field is related to education or linguistics. In other words, an applicant with a Ph.D. in chemistry might be considered preferable to one with an M.A. in English linguistics. In this particular incident, however, it was not Stephanie's credentials that were of interest to those doing the hiring, but her lack of connections. She had no financial backing, which meant that she brought no money into the university and had no one with clout to take her side against the university. She also had no strong personal relationship, or *guanxi* (connections), with any of the department or university authorities. Look for an alternative that takes guanxi into account.

4. Not a good answer. There is no reason to avoid coauthoring papers with Chinese colleagues or working closely with one colleague on a project that interests you both. On the contrary, foreign teachers are encouraged to work together with their Chinese co-workers on all sorts of projects. Even if colleagues are of opposite sexes and approximately the same age, it takes more than a professional collaboration to set tongues wagging. In fact, foreign teachers are generally assigned a "contact teacher," who looks after them: interpreting if necessary, taking care of bureaucratic issues, and making sure they are notified about banquets, outings, and meetings. Foreign teachers

often become very close friends with their contact teachers and interact with them daily.

5.   There are probably other Chinese universities where Stephanie's talents would have been better valued, but there was nothing particularly corrupt about the department she was in. Stephanie was experiencing a use of power and privilege for which her cultural conditioning had not prepared her. Look for an alternative that focuses on differences in culture, rather than on the specific university.

34 Don't Do It, Xiao Zhang

1.   There is no evidence for this answer. Liu Dehua has good relations with all of the Western teachers, not just Laura. Also, Laura has had considerable experience with Chinese people and could probably tell if someone she saw so frequently was insincere in his admiration. Finally, Laura would not likely have been offered a contract for a second year if Professor Liu had not been favorably impressed with both her teaching and her morals.

2.   It is likely that in his discussions with Zhang Qian, Professor Liu has been looking for assurances that Zhang Qian is not "marrying her passport." Many Chinese feel quite desperate to go abroad to study, and there are those who will stoop to using those who trust and love them. Nevertheless, there is no evidence that this is the case here. There is some truth to the second part of this alternative, however. In part, he is trying to assess the depth of Zhang Qian's commitment; he wants to know that this is not a frivolous infatuation before he becomes publicly involved. Find an alternative that explores this.

3.   Statistically, this alternative did not appear to be a popular one with the validation sample, and the authors agree that it is not a good answer. However, a number of people who used the incidents in their draft form felt that this was a strong alternative. Some of these people had been involved in marriages with individuals from collectivist cultures, including China. Their argument was that the majority of Chinese people in positions of authority *are* deeply suspicious of foreigners, and they view any impending Chinese-foreigner marriage as a threat to the status quo from whence they draw their authority.

The majority of our validation sample felt as the authors did, that there is no evidence for this answer within the incident. Although he may not want to marry an American or other foreigner himself, Professor Liu, with his extensive overseas experience, must certainly have encountered good marriages between Chinese and foreigners. Furthermore, we are assured that he gets along with *all* the foreign teachers, not just Laura, and it is unlikely that this would be the case if he disliked them; xenophobia, suspicion, and dislike are simply not that easy to conceal.

4. This is a good answer. In mainland Chinese culture, a department head has personal responsibility for his employees, especially for young people whose parents live in another town (Fang 1999). In a sense, Liu Dehua is in loco parentis, and it is indeed his duty to impress upon Zhang Qian that he is making a serious and perhaps very unwise choice. Professor Liu is very likely suspicious of international marriages and may know of numerous unsuccessful marriages from his past experience with his students, colleagues, and subordinates. These marriages, he will know, failed for a variety of reasons: communication difficulties, unfulfilled expectations, bureaucratic frustrations, and irreconcilable cultural differences. He will do his best to dissuade Zhang Qian from making a mistake, if a mistake it is, but he will also listen to Zhang Qian's side of things, and if he is convinced that Zhang Qian understands all the potential problems and still wishes to go through with the marriage, he will help in every way he can. Laura should not take Liu Dehua's warnings personally, because they are not directed at her as an individual. He is simply trying to protect Xiao Zhang, and she should appreciate his genuine concern for the man she loves. There should be nothing awkward about Laura's maintaining a friendly professional and personal relationship with Professor Liu.

5. This is one of two good answers. Whether or not he believes the relationship will last, Liu Dehua has a responsibility to question it, to challenge Zhang Qian's commitment. Also, it is likely that Liu Dehua has seen more than one Chinese-foreigner relationship that did not work out. Either the relationship foundered in the face of negative public opinion or ended in divorce after the couple relocated to a foreign country. If the

relationship does not work out, it will certainly be better for everyone if nothing is made public yet. There is a great deal of face at stake. Even if the authorities know about the relationship, they can continue to pretend that they do not (maintaining everyone's face) as long as Zhang Qian and Laura continue to behave discreetly.

For Liu Dehua, a loss of face (Earley 1997) is involved, no matter what. As their boss, he introduced this couple and arranged for them to work closely together, more or less alone. He will be seen by the university authorities as having acted unwisely in this, and they will certainly make sure that he knows how they feel. Furthermore, if the relationship does not work out, the loss of face will be worse for Professor Liu, since he will be seen to have failed to look out for the best interests of his young employee, exposing him to dangerous foreign ideas and allowing him to be drawn in by a foreigner whose ideas of dating, courtship, and sexual behavior are assumed to be less serious and less moral than those of the Chinese. It is important to note that Liu Dehua will still have a great deal to answer for to his superiors if Zhang Qian and Laura do get married and eventually leave China. He will be blamed for contributing to "brain drain" and for being too trusting of the foreigners he works with. He wants to be sure that he is not going to go out on a limb for this couple only to have them change their minds.

Zhang Qian will also experience some loss of face. If the relationship becomes public and then ends, he will be assumed either to be a cad or to have been duped by a wily foreigner. There are many Chinese who will make attributions like "only interested in sex," "chasing her passport," or "thinks he's too good to marry a Chinese" when the relationship becomes known. He will also become less trusted in his workplace, as co-workers will assume that he will soon be leaving for the United States with Laura.

The Chinese take romantic relationships very seriously. A person who has more than one serious commitment before marriage is generally looked upon as inconstant and unreliable. Playing the field is out of the question. If the relationship ends after it has become public, Zhang Qian may have a great deal of trouble finding a woman who is willing to marry him. He will suffer considerable humiliation. Laura, on the other hand, can return to her own country, where few potential marriage partners will look askance at a broken engagement in China.

Look, also, for another alternative that offers a slightly different cultural perspective.

35   A Right to Be Angry?

1. You are on the right track in choosing this alternative, but it is not the best answer. One of our Chinese cultural informants pointed out that while many people might become angry in these circumstances, it would not be considered wise behavior according to Chinese culture. Superiors expect deference and respect from subordinates, and overt anger interferes with these expectations. In China, as in the United States or anywhere else we know of, it is not a good idea to burn one's bridges. Former employers who can give positive recommendations about one are always an asset.

2. This is a good answer. Louise realized that she would be seeking other jobs and that it was wise to maintain good relations with employers whom she might ask to write letters of recommendation for her. Louise was aware of the company policy and may have said to herself, It's too bad that I didn't get the job, but there is a policy that gives preference to people who have passed a two-year probation. If I play it smart, I may be hired for another year-long contract, and after that I will have my two years and so will be on the preference list. Note that this thinking is consistent with individualism. People have to think through social situations and come up with a plan themselves—there is not an automatic support group that will always "be there" for people in individualistic cultures (Bhawuk 1998).

3. Dr. Bradford's behavior was appropriate in her culture, so this is not a good answer. In individualistic cultures, the information Stella and Louise received (summarized in the first and second paragraphs) was adequate. In fact, if Dr. Bradford had said much more, an American employee might grumble (out of earshot of superiors), "I'm not a child. She told me about the policy and I was given a copy of the employee handbook by the personnel department. I can read on my own!" Please choose another alternative.

4. Americans don't usually accept employment with the belief that they will work for the same organization their entire lives. Americans often change organizations, and sometimes entire career orientations, over the course of their working lives for reasons such as marriage, promotion possibilities at another organization, boredom at the current organization, desire to live in another climate, and so forth. Please choose again.

5. This is a good answer. Stella had developed a strong, personal relationship with Dr. Bradford. Recall Dr. Bradford's offer to write recommendation letters. Stella was aware of the organization's policy, but from her cultural background she expected that other factors would be as important or, perhaps, more important. In this case, Stella felt that Dr. Bradford should place their personal relationship above written organizational policy (Francesco and Gold 1998). From Dr. Bradford's point of view, she had to follow written policy or risk a lawsuit from one or more of the job applicants who had passed their probationary period. Also keep in mind that Dr. Bradford would have had to write down her reasons for not hiring a person who had passed probation. This would have been very difficult to do, and the person turned down could have appealed the decision. From Stella's viewpoint, however, all this legalistic reasoning was abstract and should have been downplayed in favor of the personal relationship. Recall incident 34 concerning the superior's discussion of marriage with his subordinate (Don't Do It, Xiao Zhang). From the Chinese viewpoint, bosses are expected to be interested in the welfare of their subordinates. They become more involved in the personal lives and emotions of their subordinates than do bosses in the United States. Bosses are expected to "look after" their subordinates, and this can be reflected in advising them on their marriages or favoring them in matters of employment within their organization.

Part Eight

Academia:
Disconfirmed Expectations

36 The Book Proposal

Wenhua Zhou from Shanghai recently received his Ph.D. in government from an Ivy League university in the United States. He wrote his dissertation on developments in Chinese economics since the death of Mao Zedong. Wenhua had become friendly with another graduate student, Judy Miller, and often sought her advice as a "cultural informant" for puzzling American social practices. Based on a recommendation from his professors back in China, Wenhua decided to seek a book publisher for his dissertation. Wenhua knew that International University Associates in New York City, a very prestigious publisher, often accepted books on modern China. He asked Judy for advice concerning how best to approach American publishers.

Judy replied, "Well, since I'm just a graduate student myself and have yet to publish a book, I'm not sure how much I can help you. I think, though, you should write a proposal describing your book in about three pages, explaining the contents to the publisher and making predictions about what type of person or institution will buy the book. Then, you should ask one of the most-published professors to review your proposal."

Wenhua followed Judy's advice and prepared a draft of such a proposal. Judy read it and then suggested that Wenhua take the proposal to Professor Brown, the author of fifteen books and a frequent consultant for a number of American publishers. Even though Professor Brown had a reputation of being approachable, Wenhua was shy about going to see him, so Judy offered to do it, since she had served as

Brown's research assistant for a year. Judy made an appointment with Professor Brown. Brown read the proposal in Judy's presence, thinking to himself, This is a good first draft. He made a number of suggestions, such as expanding the material on what types of people would be interested in the book and on moving the treatment of the content from "dissertationese" to a more readable style that would appeal to a wider audience. Brown took his pen and made a swift stroke through Wenhua's final sentence, "I hope that the prestigious editors at International University Associates will consider my unworthy submission." Noticing this swift stroke, Judy said, "I thought that was a rather charming sentence." Professor Brown replied, "Well, I don't! The faster Wenhua loses it, the better." When Judy gave the draft back to Wenhua, he couldn't understand why Professor Brown didn't like the sentence.

Why did Professor Brown cross out the sentence?

1. Professor Brown was being insensitive to Wenhua's preferred style of expressing himself, which is common in China.

2. Professor Brown felt that the proposal he was presented should have been more developed prior to the request for his suggestions.

3. Professor Brown was trying to help Wenhua achieve his goal: publication by a prestigious American press.

4. Professor Brown was trying to prepare Wenhua for the letter of rejection he would probably receive (even if Wenhua accepted all of Brown's advice).

5. Professor Brown was trying to encourage him to benefit from the natural inclinations toward collectivist thinking to which Wenhua has been exposed in China.

Explanations for The Book Proposal begin on page 209.

37 When Do Groups Form?

Dr. Philip Carey was an award-winning and prominent business professor who was asked to teach management theory during a specially arranged three-week session at Beijing University. Dr. Carey was aware of the basics of individualism and collectivism as cultural constructs, since these are frequently covered in international management courses. He was also familiar with more advanced concepts related to collectivism, such as the research finding that the target of people's collectivism has to be identified. The collective can be a family or a company or one's long-term friends (whose friendship may be based on relationships established by one's grandparents). However, relations among collectives may not be good: families may not get along and companies may have intense rivalries that make collaboration on joint projects very difficult. Dr. Carey was aware that, in China, it is not "other Chinese" to whom any one person owes allegiance as a member of a collective. Rather, the allegiance is to a family or to a company or perhaps to other residents of a village.

Given that Dr. Carey was very well known all over China because of his well-received books, fourteen Chinese scholars traveled to Beijing from all over the country to take his three-week class. Dr. Carey did not expect his students to be very cooperative with one another, since they came from different collectives, and he knew the basic point that collectivism involves allegiance to a specific group, not to some large entity such as a country. Indeed, the scholars were not very cooperative the first two weeks of class. During this time, Dr. Carey learned that the students came from different regions within the country, some of which had the reputation of being backward compared with other regions (some were from "the sticks," as people in the United States would say). In addition, while they all spoke Mandarin, they also spoke mutually unintelligible native dialects and after class would break up in pairs or small groups and speak their local dialects. Furthermore, they were from colleges and universities whose faculties competed for grants, prestige, and the attention of government leaders. Thus, Dr. Carey did not expect any signs of a collective identity among these diverse students.

During the beginning of the third week, one of the scholars became ill and had to go to the hospital. Dr. Carey learned that the students divided up the twenty-four-hour day so that one of them would be with the sick person all the time. They took notes for their ill class-mate, and they also shared notes with each other, since some had to miss class given the twenty-four-hour watch at the hospital. The students also took up a collection to pay for the sick colleague's incidental expenses associated with the hospital stay. They were certainly acting as though they were members of a collective group.

Dr. Carey said to himself, I don't understand what is going on. I thought I knew what collectivism involved. I can see that some of the students might pay a hospital visit, but I can't understand the extent of the students' efforts.

If Dr. Carey asked you for your insights, what might you say?

1. Chinese people from very different parts of the country don't always form collectives, but they are able to do so if the demands of the social context in which they find themselves make it sensible to do so.

2. Chinese people from very different parts of the country take about two weeks to get to know each other and to be comfortable with each other. Given that the student became ill during the third week, the other Chinese were comfortable enough by this time to develop a support group.

3. The student who became ill must have had the highest status among the fourteen Chinese, and so the other thirteen were expressing their deference to his status.

4. Dr. Carey was basically correct about behavior in collective societies, but his information was outdated. Cultural change since Mao's death has led to a more diffuse and general feeling of collectivism that encompasses China as a whole.

Explanations for When Do Groups Form? begin on page 210.

38   Supporting Family Members or Nepotism?

Tim Dykstal and Qu Daojiong ("Dao" to his friends) were midcareer businesspeople from Atlanta, Georgia, and Shanghai, respectively. Both were taking time off from their jobs to pursue an internationally oriented MBA degree in Hawai'i, the site of several such MBA programs that attract students from the United States, the Pacific Rim, and sometimes Europe. As part of their jobs within their organizations back home, both of which dealt with architecture and construction, Tim and Dao had both been involved with many personnel decisions.

In one class, Tim and Dao were asked to work together on a set of business case studies involving the recruitment and possible retention of entry-level managers. Based on just a glance at the cases, Tim and Dao could see that they involved choices among various candidates and that some of these candidates had family ties to company executives. In three of the cases, an outsider to the family had slightly but clearly better formal credentials and expertise than the family member—a nephew or cousin of the company executive—and so discussions of the cases were to focus on the relative weights placed on formal credentials versus kinship.

Tim had read some background material on small family businesses in China and in other parts of the world (the Chinese diaspora), and he was prepared to argue that more weight would be given to familial relations in China compared with the United States. After Tim shared this idea during one of their meetings, Dao said, "You may be working with a stereotype. Do you think a similar stereotype about you and colleagues from Atlanta, Georgia, would be accurate, given descriptions in the historical literature about old Southern families?"

After a good deal of discussion, Tim and Dao agreed that a more complex view was necessary concerning preference for hiring family members in China. This less simplistic view, however, did recognize the influence of culture. Which of the following statements seems like a reasonable generalization, keeping in mind that there will always be exceptions to generalizations? Assume that Tim or Dao has a major role in a hiring decision, that the job is an entry-level management position with significant responsibilities, and that the descriptions of applicants' qualifications are similar to those discussed in the second paragraph above.

1.   For a job in the public sector (e.g., government), Tim's cultural background more than Dao's suggests giving preference to a relative.

2. For a job in a large company engaged in intense international competition for market share with other companies, Dao's cultural background more than Tim's suggests giving preference to a relative.

3. For a teaching job in a state university, Tim's cultural background more than Dao's suggests giving preference to a relative.

4. For a job in a small family-owned firm, Dao's cultural background more than Tim's suggests giving preference to a relative.

Explanations for Supporting Family Members or Nepotism? begin on page 213.

39   Was Someone Saying No?

Dr. Xuang Xi, from an important economic planning institute in Beijing, was on a study tour of the United States. During the tour he contacted Dr. Ronald Hastings, from a similar organization in New York City, to make an appointment. Hastings, the author of several well-received books, was a highly respected economist and was considered a leading authority in the field of economic forecasting based on microeconomic predictors. During their meeting Dr. Xi invited Dr. Hastings to come to China for two months to give seminars on microeconomic variables in forecasting, with special attention to using data sets available in China.

Dr. Hastings responded, "I'm interested, but I have to check with the administrators in my organization. The organization has just received a grant that frees me from any teaching responsibilities for three years, and that's great because I can devote full time to research and writing. But I don't know the details of what the grant allows, for instance time away from New York to go to China for two months, especially since my time there will be primarily spent teaching rather than doing research. I'll check with the administrators here to get their approval."

Dr. Hastings then ended the meeting with Dr. Xi, thinking that everything had gone well. However, Dr. Hastings never heard again from Dr. Xi.

What cultural difference in the way people negotiate with each other could have been involved in this incident?

1.   Dr. Hastings was trying to be polite in communicating the message, "No, I don't want to go to China."

2.   Dr. Xi thought that Dr. Hastings was trying to be polite in communicating the message, "No, I don't want to go to China."

3.   Dr. Hastings wanted to return to the activity that gives the highest status in his profession, teaching, but he did not want to tell this to Dr. Xi directly.

4.   Dr. Xi thought that Dr. Hastings must have been able to make his own decisions about what he did with his time.

5.   Dr. Xi wanted to meet Dr. Hastings because of the networking value of interacting with a high-status person like Hastings, but he had no intention of following through with the China trip plans.

Explanations for Was Someone Saying No? begin on page 215.

40 Who Are You Trying to Fool?

Larry Wilder was enjoying his sabbatical year teaching English litera-ture at a university in central China. He was quite favorably impressed with the quality of the Chinese faculty, many of whom had studied abroad and seemed very dedicated to doing quality teaching and re-search. He was also enjoying his graduate students and occasionally visited them at their dormitories.

On one such visit to Qiu Gang, a second-year Ph.D. candidate, their conversation was interrupted by a visitor. After a brief exchange in Chinese, Qiu Gang handed the visitor an audiocassette tape, and the visitor departed. Larry inquired what the exchange had been about, and Qiu Gang casually explained that the visitor was Qiu Gang's roommate's cousin. The cousin had been accepted at a very good gradu-ate program in chemistry in the United States and had been offered a teaching assistantship contingent upon receipt of a tape of him speak-ing English. "He doesn't really speak English very well," Qiu Gang explained, "though he reads it all the time, and he did spectacularly well on the GRE, so to make sure he wouldn't lose his chance to study in the U.S., I made the tape for him."

Larry was horrified. "Don't you realize that the purpose of that tape is to make sure that he speaks English well enough so that the undergraduates he is teaching can understand him? It isn't fair to them to have a teaching assistant that can't speak English."

Qiu Gang seemed untroubled. "He's a smart guy. He'll learn to speak English really fast. And besides, I *had* to do this. His cousin is my roommate; how could I say no to my roommate? And beyond that, when my mother was sick last year, my roommate's other aunt, the sister of the chemistry student's mother, got my mother into a really good hospital in the city."

Larry was baffled and embarrassed. He had thought Qiu Gang was a really nice guy, a conscientious and creative scholar, but now he didn't know what to think. Larry found an excuse to leave, and he made a point of avoiding Qiu thereafter.

What cultural difference was the foundation of this misunderstand-ing?

1. For the Chinese, maintaining good relationships with friends is far more important than any responsibility to an abstract other.

2. The Chinese generally have no problem with being dishonest to strangers, since they cannot be caught in such lies. It's only

important to be honest with those who might catch you in your dishonesty.

3. Americans generally place a much higher value on telling the truth than the Chinese do.

4. Larry was being much too fastidious here. Qiu Gang was right that his roommate's cousin would certainly learn to speak English after he arrived in the United States and that there was no harm done.

Explanations for Who Are You Trying to Fool? begin on page 217.

41   Textbooks for All

Thom Schweitzer, an experienced English as a second language (ESL) teacher new to China, was not pleased when he realized that many of his students had copies of a familiar American textbook, but on cheap paper with black and white photographs, which in the original were colored. Clearly, the textbooks were pirated copies. He asked the students where they had gotten them, and they replied that there was a special section in the Xinhua Bookstore that sold pirated Western books at about one tenth the price of the originals.

Thom explained to the students that he thought their buying such pirated textbooks was very unfair, as it deprived the authors and the publishers of those books of their rightful profits. After his explanation, he asked his students if they would continue to buy pirated books, and they unanimously answered that they would, since that was the only way they could afford to own books in English, especially textbooks from the United States and England. Thom shook his head in disgust.

What kind of explanation might you offer Thom that would help him understand his students' point of view?

1.   For the Chinese there is no sense in which ideas or thoughts can belong to one person, so they have no concept of intellectual property rights.

2.   The students may have felt that their right to be educated superseded the right of any author or publisher to make a profit from his or her work.

3.   Many Chinese feel that the profits American authors and publishers make from the American sales of their books are sufficient, if not excessive. They feel no guilt in withholding royalties from these Americans.

4:   Chinese socialism stresses that all ideas and inventions should be shared, without economic or bureaucratic delays. This idea has been absorbed by Chinese schoolchildren for two generations.

5.   It was difficult for the Chinese students to imagine how they could possibly be hurting anyone by buying these books. The authors and publishers were too distant for their welfare to be a serious consideration.

Explanations for Textbooks for All begin on page 219.

Explanations for the Incidents in Part Eight

36   The Book Proposal

1. This is an interesting possibility. It brings up the more general question: is it best to allow people to behave according to the guidance of their own culture, or is it best to guide them into less familiar behaviors that are more appropriate in the host culture? Professor Brown might have been very sensitive and may have known exactly why Wenhua expressed himself as he did in the first draft, but he might have felt that other behaviors were appropriate given Wenhua's goals. Please try another alternative.

2. This is an interesting possibility, since it might have been true if Professor Brown were in China, behaving according to Chinese norms. However, research comparing student interactions with professors has shown that American professors are much more approachable than professors in other countries (Klineberg and Hull 1979). There is no evidence that Professor Brown resented the use of his time. Remember that he thought to himself, This is a good first draft. Professor Brown probably also realized the truth of the commonly heard saying, "Proposals, journal articles, and books are not written; they are rewritten (a large number of times.)" Please choose another alternative.

3. This is a good answer. Professor Brown was trying to help Wenhua achieve the goal of publication by a prestigious American publishing house. He knew that editors at the publishing house see large numbers of proposals where authors put forth their ideas in a dynamic, forceful way that calls attention to their first-rate qualifications (Triandis 1995b). Professor Brown knew that this style was American and was not necessarily making a judgment about its worldwide applicability; it is simply what works in America. He knew that humble statements about "unworthy proposals" would not be well received by busy editors who have many dynamic proposals competing for their attention. If Wenhua decides to accept Professor Brown's suggestions, he is simply making changes to give himself a better chance of being published in the United States.

Wenhua may still find it difficult to accept Professor Brown's suggestion. He had added that final sentence to show his modesty. Modesty is among the most important virtues to the Chinese, who believe that "real gold will ultimately shine." It doesn't help to boast about oneself. Self-promotion, marketing oneself competitively as one must do to succeed in the United States, does not come easy to a properly raised Chinese person.

4. There is no evidence for this. The incident mentioned that Professor Brown thought that Wenhua had written a good first draft. If Professor Brown thought that the proposal would not be accepted, there are other (more direct) ways that he could have told Wenhua about his concern. Professor Brown could also have suggested other alternatives, such as publication of the dissertation in a journal in article form. This is a common practice in many academic disciplines in the United States, and it is an example of "culture-specific" information that Professor Brown would be willing to share with Wenhua and Judy. Please choose another alternative.

5. Actually, Professor Brown was encouraging Wenhua to move beyond the collectivism of his socialization in China. In collectivistic societies, people often develop a highly modest style, since it is not appropriate to extol their own virtues; it is the job of their collective (uncles, bosses, former classmates) to do this (Triandis). A phrase such as "my unworthy submission" is seen as properly modest. In individualistic societies, people have to learn to extol their own virtues, since they have no collective to do this for them. One of us was told by a professor, "If you want a career in the United States, you'd better learn to blow your own horn, because no one will blow it for you." In the United States, people must develop the important social skill of letting others know of their accomplishments and talents without being viewed as highly immodest or boastful (Brislin 2000). This is a difficult skill to master even for people who have spent all their lives in the U.S. Please choose another alternative.

37 When Do Groups Form?

1. This is a good answer. As part of their socialization, people learn appropriate behaviors that can be called "social skills"

(Tobin, Wu, and Davidson 1989) These social skills can then be called upon when people find themselves in social situations where the skills are useful. Chinese from different backgrounds will not necessarily form collectives. But if the social context in which people find themselves calls for behavior typical of collectivists, they will often engage in these behaviors. In this case, a classmate became ill. A behavior typical of collectivists is to surround the sick person with supportive others. Physicians in American hospitals often comment on this fact if their patients are collectivists, such as Hispanics or Pacific Islanders: "There are so many people around it is sometimes hard to get close to my patient!"

In this incident, the social skills include staying with sick people twenty-four hours a day, taking notes for the sick person (so he or she doesn't get behind the rest of the group), taking up a collection, and so forth. One of our Chinese authors was able to describe exactly how she was socialized into the sort of behaviors that are described in this incident. When she was in elementary school, she was taught to take care of sick fellow students by taking notes. In addition, the teacher would take the students to visit the sick student in the hospital. They sang and danced to entertain the patient. After a while, she felt that she was supposed to do things like this whenever such situations occurred. When she was in high school, she remembers having done the same thing. Since, by that time, she and her fellow students were old enough to arrange trips to hospitals, they would take turns going to the hospital to keep the sick student company and to hand over the notes they had taken for the sick student. It was never a concern whether the sick student wanted their company or whether they were personally close to the sick student.

However, the issue of group formation has still not been completely addressed. An elementary or high school class is always a collective—though close bonds between individuals in the group may take time to form—whereas a short-term course is not. In addition, the students in this incident belonged to various groups that competed with each other for funding, prestige, and attention. Also, the students came from different backgrounds, and some may even have had difficulty communicating with each other due to language differences.

In Chinese culture, groups are formed in various ways. Family, friends, co-workers, classmates, and sports team members share a common bond that forms the basis of a group. This is common throughout all cultures. In China, in addition to these naturally occurring groups, there are other unique ways that groups are formed. One method is demonstrated in this incident. Although they didn't know each other very well, when circumstances demanded, they performed a set of behaviors normally expected of group members. The illness of one student galvanized the others into a group because that was the only way that they could fulfill the obligations that they had been socially conditioned to associate with this type of situation. This incident demonstrates one way that groups can be formed in Chinese society.

Of course, people in individualist cultures also learn social skills that can be called upon when the situation warrants (Triandis, Brislin, and Hui 1988). For example, assume that a person works for an organization in the United States where a positive image in the community is essential for the organization's success. For example, the organization might be a social service agency dependent on contributions from community members. It is lunchtime, and an employee named Jane is working hard on a project and so decides to eat a sandwich in her office. A person comes into the office requesting information about the organization's goals. A receptionist checks around and finds that Jane is the only person in the building who is available to speak to the visitor. The receptionist calls Jane and asks politely if she will speak with the visitor. Even though it may not be part of her formal job description, Jane will be likely to respond positively to the request and meet the visitor. Jane will then call upon social skills learned during her socialization. She will greet the visitor warmly, put the visitor at ease, tell him or her a few facts about the organization, and graciously answer some questions. Jane will never reveal the fact that she has a project she would rather be working on in her office, and she will not make the visitor feel rushed; instead, she will say a warm good-bye to the visitor, with something like "It was nice meeting you." These are carefully nurtured social skills useful in an individualistic culture, just as the social skills described in this incident are useful in a collectivistic culture.

Would other social contexts have elicited collectivist behavior? Probably. For example, if Dr. Carey had assigned projects to groups of three or four students, he would probably have been pleased with the quality of their work. Group work can often bring out the best in collectivists, since they are accustomed (owing to their socialization) to combining their efforts with those of others.

2. There is no special significance to two weeks of time together. There is no automatic or even frequently encountered move toward collectivism among diverse Chinese people based on a time frame. Please choose again.

3. This is a good guess, given the importance placed on high status in Chinese culture. However, the collective behavior described in this incident could have developed and offered its support to students of average or low status. Please choose again.

4. The behaviors learned during socialization in a culture do not change quickly, and so this possibility based on an appeal to recent social change is not the best choice. When we talk about change in a culture, we most often have to look at a period of time spanning three or more generations. Please choose again.

38   Supporting Family Members or Nepotism?

1. In the United States, government jobs are most often advertised openly, and anyone with the necessary qualifications, which are spelled out in the advertisement, can apply. If Tim hired a relative less qualified than another candidate, there are many people to whom an unsuccessful candidate could complain, and these complaints could lead to problems for the agency of government with which Tim would be involved. In fact, while this is not universal throughout American government, it is often against the law for someone like Tim to hire a relative. Please choose again.

2. While it may go through Dao's mind to hire the relative, there are several aspects of this alternative that make it part of the often untrue stereotype referred to in the incident itself. If the company is large and is engaged in intense international competition for market share, this suggests that the company may

be relatively new and thus not as subject to traditional cultural norms as are older companies. Further, if competition is intense, an executive has to hire the best person available, since the company cannot remain competitive if it hires less-qualified relatives. The pragmatics of intense competition in today's fast-moving economy will often outweigh temptations to hire relatives. There is a better alternative.

3. This is not a good answer. In the United States, jobs in public universities must be advertised. Qualified candidates then apply, and various hiring committees made up of university faculty are formed. The preferences of any one executive (e.g., a university vice president or even president) for hiring a relative will be outweighed by the committee's legal responsibility to hire the best applicant. In addition, any unsuccessful candidate has many legal steps that he or she can take, and university executives who occasionally may exert sufficient pressure to hire a relative can spend a great deal of time in court and jeopardize their own jobs.

4. Of the four alternatives, this is the most reasonable generalization. In a highly collective society like China, family serves as the basic unit in all aspects of social life. Family is part of an individual's identity (Triandis 1995b; Gao and Ting-Toomey 1998). When you fill out a personal information form in China, as you may in the course of the interview process for a new job, there will often be several questions about your parents, brothers and sisters, and close relatives. It is commonly understood among Chinese people that managers will "*ge bo zhou wang li wan*"; that is, "bend the elbow inward." This means that companies are expected to take care of their family members first. It makes good sense to keep the salaries in the family, and at the same time, family members may be expected to work harder than outsiders, since the family, as well as the individual, benefits from their efforts.

   Within small family-owned businesses, Dao's cultural conditioning would probably lead him to hire a relative. Historically in China, governments did not deliver adequate social services (health care, old-age insurance, protection of children) to the populace, so people learned to depend on their families for support and protection and as a buffer between themselves and difficulties in society. In the absence of a concept of "loyalty to an efficient government," people developed intense loyalty to their families.

But even in this case, the decision will not go in the relative's favor 100 percent of the time. In companies involved in competitive, fast-moving markets, executives may fear that the companies will be damaged if they depend on less able relatives when better-qualified candidates from outside the family have applied for responsible positions (Bhawuk 1998). The family is not well served if the company fails, and this could be an argument that an executive uses in those cases where the outsider is offered the job. If a relative is hired, it may be for a low-level job, where poor work will probably not have much of an impact on the company. On the other hand, it can often be assumed that even a slightly less-qualified relative may be the better choice as an employee, since a member of the collective has a more direct stake in the success or failure of the enterprise and would be expected to work longer and harder than a nonrelative.

39   Was Someone Saying No?

1. While appealing to a vague bureaucratic authority as an excuse for not doing something is always a possibility, that is not what Dr. Hastings was doing here. Also, keep in mind that he was surprised that there was not a follow-up communication from Dr. Xi. An American could tell that Dr. Hastings was indeed interested in Dr. Xi's proposal. If he had wished to refuse the offer, Dr. Hastings would most likely have expressed his regrets directly, for example, "I'm sorry. That sounds interesting, but the terms of my grant probably won't allow me to travel to China." He could have used the terms of the grant to excuse himself, but he would have made his refusal less ambiguous. Please choose another alternative.

2. This is the better of two good answers. From Dr. Xi's point of view, Dr. Hastings was quite clearly saying no in a polite way (Brislin and Hui 1993). When Dr. Xi heard Dr. Hastings talk about administrative burdens that needed to be faced, he may have thought Dr. Hastings was trying to be polite and to communicate in an indirect manner by alluding to all the adminis-

trators who would eventually say no. Dr. Xi probably recognized this as a way that he, himself, would say no under similar circumstances. This explanation becomes even clearer when combined with another that also contributes to a fuller understanding of the incident. Please look for this other good answer.

3. Actually, and perhaps unfortunately, teaching is not the activity that leads to high status in the development of careers such as that of Dr. Hastings in the United States. Research and extensive writing lead to prestigious careers. Also, Dr. Hastings seems to be pleased to be relieved of teaching duties. There is no indication that he is eager to return to teaching. Please choose again.

4. Although the authors think this is a strong possibility, it was not judged as a likely explanation by the validation sample. Nevertheless, it is worth considering. Some Chinese, and Americans as well, are very sensitive about their social status (Earley 1997). In the rest of this explanation, we are assuming that Dr. Xi is one of those highly esteemed professionals who take the privileges of his position seriously. From Dr. Xi's point of view, then, someone with Dr. Hastings' status should have been able to make his own decisions about the use of his time and should not have had to receive permission from a set of administrators. This is one benefit of high status (from Dr. Xi's point of view)—a certain amount of freedom from petty bureaucracies! This should have been especially true (again, from Dr. Xi's viewpoint), given that Dr. Hastings was from a country where people have a great deal of freedom. How could people be free if they had to clear their time with petty bureaucracies? From Dr. Hastings' point of view, on the other hand, there were many legal restrictions on how grant money in the United States could be spent and he did indeed have to check with administrators about that. When Dr. Hastings talked about administrators, however, Dr. Xi heard a different message. Another alternative deals with this message. Please look for this other alternative.

5. There are always individuals who abuse visits to other countries and make promises on which they cannot possibly deliver. However, this is not so common as to be considered part of Chinese culture. In addition, if Dr. Xi knew about the value of

networking in the United States (as implied in the wording of this alternative), he would know that his reputation would become one of total disrespect if he did not follow through on promises. Please choose another alternative.

40   Who Are You Trying to Fool?

1.   This is a good answer. The Chinese are collectivists and therefore feel that maintaining and strengthening relationships among those within the collective are crucial (Triandis 1995b). Qiu Gang naturally felt that not disappointing his roommate and his roommate's family, who were part of his collective, was very important. Furthermore, they were part of his *guanxi* (connections) network (Luo and Chen 1996; Tsang 1998). Recall, also, that he was in guanxi debt to them for helping get treatment for his ill mother. Their needs were certainly much more important to him than the potential problems of some bunch of unseen, unknown undergraduates in the United States. Qiu Gang's debt was clearly to those he knew, not to some distant persons he did not know.

Qiu Gang certainly realized that his behavior was unethical, in the abstract, but his personal obligations to the people close to him so strongly outweighed that abstraction as to make it all but irrelevant. The Chinese say "*Wei pengyou liang lei chadao*," which literally means "For my friends I am willing to stab both of my own sides with a knife."

Since this incident really bothered Larry, he might have been interested to know that one of us has convinced a Chinese friend not to do this type of thing again, except in the most pressing circumstances. Larry could have drawn an analogy with a hypothetical situation that would affect people within Qiu Gang's own collective. For example, if Qiu Gang's department hired a U.S. citizen to teach linguistics or language to the same students Qiu Gang teaches, and the person, when he arrived, was discovered not only to have no experience teaching linguistics or English as a foreign language, but also to be a native speaker of German with a very heavy accent, Qiu Gang would feel angry that his students had been cheated.

2.   Without some other motivation, the Chinese are no more likely than people of any other country to be gratuitously dishonest.

It's not so much a matter of being caught as the motivation for being dishonest. In this particular case, however, Qiu Gang was probably not concerned with honesty or dishonesty, but only with helping a friend in need. To Qiu Gang, the chance to enable a member of his collective to have a great opportunity like studying in an excellent U.S. graduate program was not to be passed up. The *possible* harm to his friend's cousin's *potential* undergraduate students was too remote to be considered.

If he did think about it, Qiu Gang would probably place the making of this tape along a continuum very close to exaggerating the importance of one's involvement in activities or enhancing the status of one's position on applications, a form of half-truth at which Americans are considerably more adept than Chinese applicants.

3. This is not a good answer. What is understood as an acceptable lie or half-truth differs a great deal from culture to culture. Larry and Qiu Gang disagreed about the severity of this particular deceptive behavior. Many Chinese coming to the United States, on the other hand, are taken in by fraudulent advertising schemes, those that most people of the same age and educational background raised in American culture find transparent. Many Chinese find it shocking that Americans take it for granted that they will be lied to in advertisements and that the language of advertising is rife with intentionally misleading language. Another example of "lies" that irritate Chinese visitors but which Americans take for granted is the "I'll call you" social promise, where there is no intention to get in touch at all, or worse, "Let me think about it and call you back" (see Are Ethical Issues Involved? pages 157–58 and 169–70 for more discussion of this issue).

4. This is not a very good answer. There was a very good chance that Qiu Gang's roommate's cousin would have been a terrible, incomprehensible teaching assistant well into his stay in the United States. Possibly not, but it was likely. Larry had good reason to be upset—an injustice was being done—but Qiu Gang also had good reasons for what he did. Look for another answer that will give the culturally influenced reasons.

41   Textbooks for All

1. This answer should certainly be part of your thinking about the issues raised, though it is overstated, given that intellectual property rights have been widely discussed in the international media and that Chinese intellectuals have access to this coverage. The concept of individual ownership of ideas and texts is peculiarly Western and is indeed rather difficult for many Chinese to grasp. It is certainly difficult to explain to Chinese students that even though their ideas are exactly the same as a published author's ideas, they cannot simply use his or her words as if they were their own. That is not, however, the main issue here. It was not so difficult for the Chinese students to understand that the person who did the work of putting together a textbook—writing or collecting text and pictures and editing—should be paid for the work. However, given the choice between going without the book or buying a copy for which the original author and publisher received no compensation, it would be a very rare Chinese student who would see any virtue in going without the book.

   Patent and copyright infringement in China has become a big concern within the international community. In 1990 the Chinese government actually enacted a copyright law under pressure from countries like Japan and the United States. However, the situation has not changed much. This is not something that the government can deal with simply by enacting rules and regulations, because it is deeply embedded in the Chinese culture.

   The Confucian idea that individuals should sacrifice personal profit in order to benefit the group has led the Chinese to hold copyrights, used by authors to secure private profit, in less regard than in the West (Overholt 1993). Confucianism is concerned primarily with the moral development of people (Tu 1989) and the accepted modes of behavior in a civilized state (Lazar 1996). It stresses government by education, persuasion, and moral example. Imitation—of teachers, leaders, parents, and other moral authority figures—leads to a harmonious society. According to Confucianism, a formal legal system serves only to make people litigious and self-interested. Morality leads to social order, and group order is more important than individual desires. Confucianism and traditional Chinese culture also placed a strong emphasis on societal good rather than the pursuit of personal rewards. As early as the Qing Dynasty (211 B.C.), the individual pursuit of economic gain was seen as a threat to the state and was actively discouraged. Copyright royalties were believed to threaten social equality by enriching authors at the expense of society.

Chinese intellectuals rely on historical developments in literature, fine arts, and calligraphy to a greater degree than do Westerners. This appreciation of the past is also reflected in the Chinese view of copying as a way of paying a great compliment to an author (Lazar). Essentially, Chinese intellectuals feel that the works of prior authors and artists should be available for scholars and artists to build on.

2. A good answer, but not the best one. It is probably erroneous to assume that the students were consciously and directly setting up their right to be educated against the right of authors and publishers to make profits, though, if pressed, they might argue that the right to learn supersedes anyone's right to profit. Their own needs would certainly outweigh the needs of anyone so distant, anyone to whom they had no personal obligations. However, if asked, they would probably agree that the author and publisher have a right to some compensation. They might argue that they would buy an original, copyrighted textbook *if they could afford it,* which of course they cannot. Since they cannot afford it, the question becomes an empty one.

    In fact, even now there are few Western books available that are sold through normal distribution channels. For example, popular magazines like *Time* and *Newsweek* are sold only at five-star hotels, where many foreign tourists stay but where Chinese college students would not be welcomed. The pirated English books might not only have been the only affordable resources for the students; they might have been the *only* resources, affordable or not.

3. This answer is on the right track, but it falls short. It is doubtful if anything as concrete as "withholding royalties" ever entered these students' minds. They needed the book; their friends needed the book; and someone provided a copy that they could afford. It is likely true that the students felt no guilt, and they

might even have said "Those publishers are rich enough," but they would not have suggested that the authors and publishers had no right to a profit. However, whether the publishers made a profit or not was no concern of theirs, since those people were too far removed from their lives and the collective of people whose welfare was their responsibility. Look for an answer that reflects this aspect of Chinese culture.

4. This is not a good answer. Socialism has indeed been taught to Chinese children for two generations, but the cultural issue being discussed here goes back further than that. Many would argue that socialism caught on precisely because of the collectivist nature of Chinese society.

5. This is the best answer. As we have seen in many of the other incidents, the welfare of those in one's immediate collective is of paramount importance. To these Chinese students, it was an obvious good that they and their classmates had access to the best possible textbooks. It was a far less obvious evil that they were depriving an unknown, not to mention foreign, person of whatever pittance he or she would have gotten from the sale of an additional book.

Appendix

Culture Assimilators: Evaluation Research

Culture assimilator-based training programs have been the focus of more research than any other cross-cultural training method. Extensive reviews have been prepared by a number of scholars (Albert 1995; Brislin and Yoshida 1994; Cushner and Brislin 1996; Cushner and Landis 1996; Triandis 1995b; Triandis, Kurowski, and Gelfand 1994), and these sources should be consulted for longer discussions of the points raised here. To introduce the topic of evaluation research, four documented outcomes of culture assimilators will be reviewed here: (1) increased complexity of people's thinking, (2) better problem solving, (3) improved relations with hosts, and (4) introduction to behaviors that are appropriate in the host culture.

Increased Complexity in Thinking. The most commonly found outcome of assimilator training is that people think in a more complex manner about intercultural interactions (Bhawuk 1998; Bhawuk and Brislin 2000; Cushner 1989; Weldon et al. 1975). After training, people do not make attributions about the misunderstandings depicted in critical incidents based on the first thoughts that come to their minds. Rather, they think more carefully and learn to make *isomorphic attributions.* This term, commonly heard in discussions of cross-cultural training (Triandis 1995b; Triandis, Kurowski, and Gelfand), means that trainees learn to make the same attributions as people in other cultures. Rather than impose their own attribution learned in their own culture, trainees learn that there is another viewpoint that must be taken into account, the viewpoint of the host country. In the critical incident presented earlier (page 9), for example, Norman Tate would learn that Mr. Lu's viewpoint has to be understood.

Trainees can learn to analyze critical incidents in very complex ways. Dharm P. S. Bhawuk (1998) developed a theory-based culture assimilator that had the goal of introducing complex (but very helpful) theoretical concepts. A reasonable conclusion from Bhawuk's study is that trainees can be taught to think in more complex ways by introducing them to well-established concepts from cross-cultural research and asking them to apply these concepts to difficult critical incidents. In this way trainees' thinking moved away from making simple snap judgments based on experiences only in their own culture to retrieving information about complex concepts and applying them to make isomorphic attributions.

Better Problem Solving. Even with extensive experiences in cultures other than their own, people can never be prepared for every intercultural interaction they will have. The issue is not one of avoiding problems but of having effective ways of dealing with them when they arise. Cushner (1989) found that people who had participated in assimilator training developed better problem-solving skills than people who had not. The major reason is the behavior that logically follows from the greater complexity of thinking already discussed. If people can take into account the viewpoint of their hosts, they are more likely to develop a workable solution to problems and to act on them.

Improved Relations with Hosts. Studies have shown that compared with untrained people, individuals trained with assimilators are looked upon by hosts in a more favorable manner (O'Brien and Plooj 1977; Weldon et al.). The research approach is especially interesting. A group of assimilator-trained people are asked to a social gathering that hosts from the target culture attend. "Untrained" people also attend, but the hosts do not know who has received training and who has not. People interact in a manner typical of social gatherings: talking, telling stories, eating, moving around and meeting different people, introducing people not known to each other, and so forth. The researchers later ask the hosts who they enjoyed interacting with and who seemed culturally sensitive. Keeping one caveat in mind (to be discussed in the next paragraph), hosts name more trained than untrained people as enjoyable and sensitive individuals.

The one caveat is that trainees need time between the end of training and the beginning of the social gathering. This time period does not have to be long—a few hours is enough—but it is necessary for people to think about the content of training, to relax about their upcoming intercultural interactions, and to look forward to meeting culturally different others. If people move immediately from the training site to the social gathering, they can be very stiff and overly formal. They have learned that cultural differences have an impact, and they may worry about offending others. If they are overly formal and careful in their chats with hosts, they will not always communicate sensitivity and interest. If, however, they have time to relax and calm down after culture assimilator training, they are preferred by hosts over untrained people.

The Introduction to New Behaviors. In their own cultures, people develop habitual ways of behaving so as to attain their goals in a variety of social settings. An important part of successful adjustment to other cultures is the identification and adoption of other, sometimes new, behaviors that are more culturally appropriate. Culture assimilators can introduce and encourage these behaviors, and adoption of these behaviors can sometimes lead to better job performance. In a study of American medical volunteers assigned to introduce preventive health practices in Honduras, sojourners who had received culture assimilator training were able to inoculate more hosts against prevalent diseases than untrained sojourners (O'Brien, Fiedler, and Hewett 1971). Part of the assimilator training dealt with the cultural issue of the prohibition against young people touching older people in Honduras. Because many of the volunteers were younger than hosts who might be inoculated, this presented a problem. Trained volunteers learned that they should give the inoculations in a confident manner and should show respect to elders, thus gaining the trust of the hosts. Given this trust, the hosts would overlook any cultural faux pas as long as the value of the inoculations had been communicated to them. The finding of increased job performance has to be carefully qualified to avoid making false promises. Our conclusion is that culture assimilator training can improve job performance when (1) there are culturally appropriate behaviors that contribute to job performance, (2) these behaviors can be introduced and explained in the training materials, and (3) people are willing to adopt these behaviors in their interactions with hosts.

The Criteria of Success and Culture Assimilators

The type of information presented in a culture assimilator can contribute to success on an overseas assignment according to the four criteria of success introduced on pages 4–5. The first criterion is that people enjoy their sojourns. Culture assimilators can give people information about another culture so that they become noticeably less frustrated when they encounter cultural differences. They can learn that such differences are to be expected and can often be *understood,* given the links between critical incidents and explanatory concepts discussed earlier. If people are less frustrated, expect to encounter differences, and can understand the reasons for at least some of the differences, the chances of an enjoyable sojourn are increased.

The second criterion is that hosts respond positively to the sojourners. The research reviewed here on pages 223–25 directly addressed this issue: after trainees had an opportunity to think about the information they learned, hosts preferred assimilator-trained people to untrained individuals (O'Brien and Plooj; Weldon et al). Trained people were able to communicate an appreciation of culture and cultural differences, showed respect to hosts, and were culturally sensitive in their interactions with hosts. Hosts appreciated these behaviors and responded positively.

When people learn about at least some of the culturally appropriate behaviors associated with their goals, they can actually engage in these behaviors and consequently increase their chances of attaining their goals. In the study reviewed on the previous page, medical workers wanted to accomplish the goal of introducing preventive health practices. They learned culturally appropriate behaviors associated with this goal, and they were successful if they integrated these behaviors into their everyday interactions with hosts. In the critical incident involving Norman Tate and Lu Kang (page 9), we argue that Norman would increase his chances of goal accomplishment if he changed his preferred behavior (telephoning directly) to the use of intermediaries.

The fourth criterion is stress reduction. One of the contributors to stress during overseas assignments is the feeling that "I am the only one experiencing these negative feelings and frustrations." Culture assimilator training can change this self-assessment: many if not all people are occasionally frustrated in their experiences abroad and are tempted to engage in very negative thinking. When people read multiple incidents that depict multiple possible misunderstandings, they move away from the belief that only unsuccessful people experience stress. Instead they learn that a certain amount of stress, summarized by the term *culture shock*, is inevitable (Brislin and Yoshida).

References

Albert, Rosita D. 1995. "The Intercultural Sensitizer/Culture Assimilator as a Cross-Cultural Training Method." In *Intercultural Sourcebook: Cross-Cultural Training Methods,* vol. 1, edited by Sandra M. Fowler and Monica G. Mumford, 157–67. Yarmouth, ME: Intercultural Press.

———. 1983. "The Intercultural Sensitizer or Culture Assimilator: A Cognitive Approach." In *Handbook of Intercultural Training: Issues in Training Methodology,* vol. 2, edited by Dan Landis and Richard Brislin, 186–217. Elmsford, NY: Pergamon.

Althen, Gary. 1995. *The Handbook of Foreign Student Advising.* Rev. ed. Yarmouth, ME: Intercultural Press.

Bhawuk, Dharm P. S. 1998. "The Role of Culture Theory in Cross-Cultural Training: A Multidimensional Study of Culture-Specific, Culture-General, and Culture Theory-Based Assimilators." *Journal of Cross-Cultural Psychology* 29: 630–55.

Bhawuk, Dharm P. S., and Richard Brislin. 2000. "Cross-Cultural Training: A Review." *Applied Psychology: An International Review* 49, no. 1: 162–91.

Bond, Michael H., ed. 1986. *The Psychology of the Chinese People.* New York: Oxford.

Brake, Terence, Danielle M. Walker, and Thomas Walker. 1995. *Doing Business Internationally: The Guide to Cross-Cultural Success.* Burr Ridge, IL: Irwin.

Brislin, Richard. W. 2000. *Understanding Culture's Influence on Behavior.* 2d ed. Fort Worth, TX: Harcourt Brace.

Brislin, Richard W., and C. Harry Hui. 1993. "The Preparation of Managers for Overseas Assignments: The Case of China." In *International Business in China,* edited by Oded Shenkar and Lane Kelley, 233–58. London: Routledge.

Brislin, Richard W., and Tomoko Yoshida. 1994. *Intercultural Communication Training: An Introduction*. Thousand Oaks, CA: Sage.

Cateora, Philip, and John Graham. 1999. *International Marketing*. 10th ed. Boston: Irwin/McGraw-Hill.

Chinese Culture Connection. 1987. "Chinese Values and the Search for Culture-Free Dimensions of Culture." *Journal of Cross-Cultural Psychology* 18: 143–64.

Choi, Incheol, Richard E. Nisbett, and Ara Norenzayan. 1999. "Causal Attribution across Cultures: Variation and Universality." *Psychological Bulletin* 125: 47–63.

Cushner, Kenneth. 1989. "Assessing the Impact of a Culture-General Assimilator." *International Journal of Intercultural Relations* 13: 125–46.

Cushner, Kenneth, and Richard Brislin. 1996. *Intercultural Interactions: A Practical Guide*. 2d ed. Thousand Oaks, CA: Sage.

Cushner, Kenneth, and Dan Landis. 1996. "The Intercultural Sensitizer." In *Handbook of Intercultural Training*, 2d ed., edited by Dan Landis and Rabi S. Bhagat, 185–202. Thousand Oaks, CA: Sage.

Dorfman, Peter. 1996. "International and Cross-Cultural Leadership." In *Handbook for International Management Research*, edited by Betty Punnett and Oded Shenkar, 267–349. Cambridge, MA: Blackwell.

Eagly, Alice, and Shelly Chaiken. 1998. "Attitude Structure and Function." In *The Handbook of Social Psychology*, 4th ed., vol. 1, edited by Daniel Gilbert, Susan Fiske, and Gardner Lindzey, 269–322. New York: McGraw-Hill.

Earley, P. Christopher. 1997. *Face, Harmony, and Social Structure: An Analysis of Organizational Behavior across Cultures*. New York: Oxford University Press.

———. 1989. "Social Loafing and Collectivism: A Comparison of the United States and the People's Republic of China." *Administrative Science Quarterly* 34: 565–81.

Fang, Tony. 1999. *Chinese Business Negotiating Style*. Thousand Oaks, CA: Sage.

Fiedler, Fred E., Terence Mitchell, and Harry C. Triandis. 1971. "The Culture Assimilator: An Approach to Cross-Cultural Training." *Journal of Applied Psychology* 55: 95–102.

Fiske, Alan, Shinobu Kitayama, Hazel Markus, and Richard E. Nisbett. 1998. "The Cultural Matrix of Social Psychology." In *The Handbook of Social Psychology*, 4th ed., vol. 2, edited by Daniel Gilbert,

Susan Fiske, and Gardner Lindzey, 357–411. New York: McGraw-Hill.

Fowler, Sandra M., and Monica G. Mumford, eds. 1999. *Intercultural Sourcebook: Cross-Cultural Training Methods,* vol. 2. Yarmouth, ME: Intercultural Press.

Fowler, Sandra M., and Monica G. Mumford, eds. 1995. *Intercultural Sourcebook: Cross-Cultural Training Methods,* vol. 1. Yarmouth, ME: Intercultural Press.

Francesco, Anne Marie, and Barry Gold. 1998. *International Organizational Behavior.* Upper Saddle River, NJ: Prentice-Hall.

Fukuyama, Francis. 1995. *Trust: The Social Virtues and the Creation of Prosperity.* New York: Free Press.

Gao, Ge, and Stella Ting-Toomey. 1998. *Communicating Effectively with the Chinese.* Thousand Oaks, CA: Sage.

Gao, Guopei. "International Business in China." 1993. In *International Business in China,* edited by Oded Shenkar and Lane Kelley, 225–32. London: Routledge.

Hall, Edward T. [1966] 1982. *The Hidden Dimension.* Reprint, New York: Anchor/Doubleday.

Hofstede, Geert. 1980. *Culture's Consequences: International Differences in Work-Related Values.* Newbury Park, CA: Sage.

Hofstede, Geert, and Michael H. Bond. 1988. "Confucius & Economic Growth: New Trends in Culture's Consequences." *Organizational Dynamics* 16, no. 4: 4–21.

Hsu, Francis L. K. 1981. *American and Chinese: Passage to Differences.* 3d ed. Honolulu, HI: University Press of Hawaii.

Hu Wenzhong, and Cornelius Grove. 1999. *Encountering the Chinese: A Guide for Americans.* 2d ed. Yarmouth, ME: Intercultural Press.

Hui, C. Harry. 1990. "Work Attitudes, Leadership Styles, and Managerial Behaviors in Different Cultures." In *Applied Cross-Cultural Psychology,* edited by Richard Brislin, 186–208. Newbury Park, CA: Sage.

Hui, C. Harry, and Chung Luk. 1997. "Industrial/Organizational Psychology." In *Handbook of Cross-Cultural Psychology: Behavior and Applications,* 2d ed., vol. 3, edited by John W. Berry, Marshall H. Segall, and Cigdem Kagitcibasi, 371–411. Boston: Allyn and Bacon.

Kagitcibasi, Cigdem. 1997. "Individualism and Collectivism." In *Handbook of Cross-Cultural Psychology: Behavior and Applications,* 2d ed., vol. 3, edited by John W. Berry, Marshall H. Segall, and Cigdem Kagitcibasi, 1–49. Boston: Allyn and Bacon.

Kelley, Lane, and Yadong Luo. 1999. *China 2000: Emerging Business Is-sues.* Thousand Oaks, CA: Sage.

Klineberg, Otto, and W. Frank Hull. 1979. *At a Foreign University: An International Study of Adaptation and Coping.* New York: Praeger.

Kohls, L. Robert, with Herbert L. Brussow. 1995. *Training Know-How for Cross-Cultural and Diversity Trainers.* Duncanville, TX: Adult Learning Systems.

Landis, Dan, and Rabi S. Bhagat, eds. 1996. *Handbook of Intercultural Training.* 2d ed. Thousand Oaks, CA: Sage.

Landis, Dan, and Richard W. Brislin, eds. 1983. *Handbook of Intercultural Training* (3 vols.). Elmsford, NY: Pergamon.

Lazar, June Cohan. 1996. "Protecting Ideas and Ideals: Copyright Law in the People's Republic of China." *Law and Policy in International Business* 27, no. 4: 1185–211.

Lee, Kam-Hon, and Thamis Wing-Chun Lo. 1993. "American Business People's Perceptions of Marketing and Negotiating in the People's Republic of China. In *International Business in China,* edited by Oded Shenkar and Lane Kelley, 208–24. London: Routledge.

Levine, Robert. 1997. *A Geography of Time.* New York: Basic Books.

Ling, Wen-quan. 1989. "Pattern of Leadership Behavior Assessment in China." *Psychologia: An International Journal of Psychology in the Orient* 32: 129–34.

Luo, Yadong, and Min Chen. 1996. "Managerial Implications of Guanxi-Based Business Strategies." *Journal of International Management* 2: 293–316.

Markus, Hazel, and Shinobu Kitayama. 1991. "Culture and the Self: Implications for Cognition, Emotion, and Motivations." *Psychological Review* 98: 224–53.

Maslow, Abraham H. 1970. *Motivation and Personality.* 2d ed. New York: Harper and Row.

Noe, Robert M. 1999. *Employee Training and Development.* Boston: Irwin/McGraw-Hill.

O'Brien, Gordon E., Fred E. Fiedler, and Tom Hewett. 1971. "The Effects of Programmed Culture Training upon the Performance of Volunteer Medical Teams in Central America." *Human Relations* 24: 209–31.

O'Brien, Gordon E. and Daniel Plooj. 1977. "Development of Culture Training Manuals for Medical Workers with Pitjantiatjara Aboriginals: The Relative Effects of Critical Incident and Prose Training upon Knowledge, Attitudes, and Motivation." In *Ab-*

original Cognition: Retrospect and Prospect, edited by George Kearney and Donald McElwain, 383–96. Canberra: Australian Institute of Aboriginal Studies.

Overholt, William H. 1993. *The Rise of China: How Economic Reform Is Creating a New Superpower*. New York: Norton.

Pruitt, Dean G. 1998. "Social Conflict." In *The Handbook of Social Psychology*, 4th ed., vol. 2, edited by Daniel Gilbert, Susan Fiske, and Gardner Lindzey, 470–503. New York: McGraw-Hill.

Pye, Lucian W. 1992. *Chinese Negotiating Style: Commercial Approaches and Cultural Principles*. New York: Quorum Books.

———. 1982. *Chinese Commercial Negotiating Style*. Cambridge, MA: Oelgeschlager, Gunn and Hain.

Salzman, Michael S. 1990. "The Construction of an Intercultural Sensitizer for Training Non-Navajo Personnel." *Journal of American Indian Education* 30, no. 1: 25–33.

Schoonhals, Martin. 1994. "Encouraging Talk in Chinese Classrooms." *Anthropology and Education Quarterly* 25: 399–412.

Shenkar, Oded, ed. 1990. *Organization and Management in China 1979–1990*. Armonk, NY: M. E. Sharpe.

Shenkar, Oded, and Simcha Ronen. 1993. "The Cultural Context of Negotiations: The Implications of Chinese Interpersonal Norms." In *International Business in China*, edited by Oded Shenkar and Lane Kelley, 191–207. London: Routledge.

Stewart, Sally, and Chong Chung Him. 1990. "Chinese Winners: Views of Senior PRC Managers on the Reasons for Their Success." *International Studies of Management and Organizations* (issue edited by Oded Shenkar, Organization and Management in China, 1979–1990) 20, nos. 1–2: 57–68.

Tobin, Joseph Jay, David Y. H. Wu, and Dana H. Davidson. 1989. *Preschool in Three Cultures: Japan, China, and the United States*. New Haven, CT: Yale University Press.

Tomlinson, Richard. 1999. "China's Reform: Now Comes the Hard Part." *Fortune*, 1 March, 158–64.

Triandis, Harry. 1995a. "Culture-Specific Assimilators." In *Intercultural Sourcebook: Cross-Cultural Training Methods*, vol. 1, edited by Sandra M. Fowler and Monica G. Mumford, 179–86. Yarmouth, ME: Intercultural Press.

———. 1995b. *Individualism and Collectivism*. Boulder, CO: Westview Press.

Triandis, Harry C., Richard W. Brislin, and C. Harry Hui. 1988. "Cross-Cultural Training across the Individualism-Collectivism Divide." *International Journal of Intercultural Relations* 12: 269–89.

Triandis, Harry C., Lois L. Kurowski, and Michele J. Gelfand. 1994. "Workplace Diversity." In *Handbook of Industrial and Organizational Psychology,* vol. 4, 2d ed., edited by Harry C. Triandis, Marvin D. Dunnette, and Leaetta M. Hough, 769–827. Palo Alto, CA: Consulting Psychologists Press.

Tsang, Eric W. K. 1998. "Can Guanxi Be a Source of Sustained Competitive Advantage for Doing Business in China?" *Academy of Management Executive* 12, no. 2: 64–73.

Tu, Weiming. 1989. *The Way, Learning, and Politics: Essays on the Confucian Intellectual.* Singapore: Institute of East Asian Philosophies.

Weldon, David E., Donal Carlston, A. Kent Rissman, Leonard Slobodin, and Harry Triandis. 1975. "A Laboratory Test of the Effects of Culture Assimilator Training." *Journal of Personality and Social Psychology* 32: 300–310.

Wight, Albert R. 1995. "The Critical Incident as a Training Tool." In *Intercultural Sourcebook: Cross-Cultural Training Methods,* vol. 1, edited by Sandra M. Fowler and Monica G. Mumford, 127–40. Yarmouth, ME: Intercultural Press.

Zhu, Cherrie Jiuhua. 1999. "Major Emerging Issues in Human Resource Management." In *China 2000: Emerging Business Issues,* edited by Lane Kelley and Yadong Luo, 333–63. Thousand Oaks, CA: Sage.

Zhu, Yunxia. 1999. *Business Communication in China.* Commack, NJ: Nova Science.

About the Authors

Mary Margaret (Knapp) Wang was born and grew up in Wisconsin. She taught English at Nanjing University in China from 1980–1983 and again from 1989–1992. At the time of the initial stages of the writing of this book, Mary was on a fellowship from the East-West Center of the University of Hawai'i, which honored her with a research award for this project. She has taught ESL at the University of Wisconsin and is a Mandarin medical interpreter. Her M.A. is in ESL from the University of Hawai'i.

Richard W. Brislin was born and grew up in New England. He is a widely published and highly respected expert in the field of cross-cultural training. He is now at the College of Business Administration, University of Hawai'i, where he directs the Ph.D. program in international management. His Ph.D. is in psychology from The Pennsylvania State University. He is the author of *Understanding Culture's Influence on Behavior*, coauthor with Kenneth Cushner of *Intercultural Interactions: A Practical Guide*, and coeditor with Kenneth Cushner and Tomoko Yoshida Isogai of *Improving Intercultural Interactions: Modules for Cross-Cultural Training Programs*.

Wei-zhong Wang was born and grew up in rural Jiangsu Province in Eastern China. He graduated from and later taught English at Nanjing University. He emigrated to the U.S. in 1992, shortly after marriage to Mary. Wei-zhong has worked in retail sales and as an interpreter; he is currently doing computer technical support and building websites for the University of Wisconsin.

David Williams was born and grew up in Idaho and spent two years in Taiwan on a mission for the Church of Jesus Christ of Latter-Day Saints.

While working on the materials in this book, he was studying business administration with an emphasis on international business and was on a fellowship from the East-West Center of the University of Hawai'i.

Julie Haiyan Chao was born and grew up in Shanghai, China, and has worked in the fashion industry in Hong Kong. She obtained a two-year leave of absence from her position in Hong Kong, obtained an MBA from the University of Hawai'i (where she worked closely with Dr. Brislin), and has returned to her organization in Hong Kong.

Index of Incidents According to Themes and Concepts

This index will chiefly be of use to trainers. Not all of the incidents listed under each heading have that theme as their particular focus, but the incident does include some aspect of that concept.

Breinigsville, PA USA
24 November 2010
249841BV00008B/1/A

9 781877 864810